SUE LAWRENCE

A Cook's tour of SCOTLAND

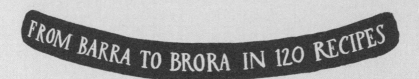

FROM BARRA TO BRORA IN 120 RECIPES

headline

Also by Sue Lawrence:
Sue Lawrence's Book of Baking
Sue Lawrence's Scottish Kitchen
Scots Cooking

First published in 2006
by HEADLINE BOOK PUBLISHING

1

ISBN 0 7553 1417 4

Cataloguing in Publication Data is available from the British Library

Art direction by Smith & Gilmour, London
Food styling by Maxine Clark
Photography by Dan Jones
Designed by Smith & Gilmour, London
Typeset in New Clarendon and Belizio by Smith & Gilmour, London
Colour reproduction by Spectrum Colour Ltd, Ipswich
Printed and bound in Italy by Canale & C.S.p.A

Headline's policy is to use papers that are natural, renewable and recyclable
products and made from wood grown in sustainable forests. The logging
and manufacturing processes are expected to conform to the environmental
regulations of the country of origin.

HEADLINE BOOK PUBLISHING
A division of Hodder Headline
338 Euston Road
London NW1 3BH

www.headline.co.uk
www.hodderheadline.com

Contents

For my dear friend and cousin-in-law Sue Hadden,
one of Scotland's best soup-makers.

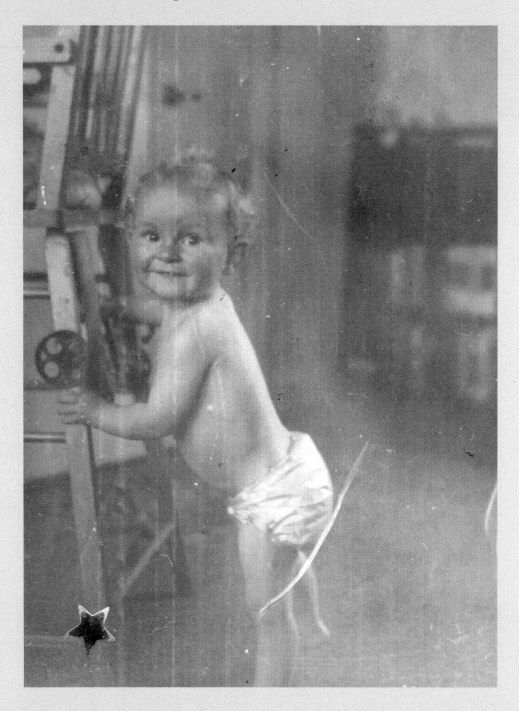

Acknowledgements

Laura Alexander, Craig Archibald, Lesley Banks, Lesley Bell, Gordon Bennett, Toni Blacklock, Joanna Blythman, Gaven Borthwick, Dave Broom, Mike Callender, Iain Campbell, Hilary Cochran, Mary Coghill, Mary Contini, David Craig, Jonathan Crombie, Jo Currie, Linda and Jim Dick, Clarissa Dickson-Wright, Ewan Donaldson, Paul Doull, Anne and Ronnie Eunson, Barbara Foulkes, Olive Geddes, John Gordon, Barry Graham, Lorna Grains, Christine Hall, Debbie and Dave Hammond, Margaret Horn, David Ismail, Isabel Johnson, Caroline Keith, George Lawrie, Dolina Macdonald, Jane and Iain Macdonald, Willie Macdonald, Netta MacDougall, Billy Mcfarlane, Dods Macfarlane, Jim McFarlane, Amanda Maclaren, Iain and Margaret Macleod, Meg McMillan, Jo Macsween, John Mellis, Sandy Milne, Gary Moore, Dafydd Morris, Sandy and Heather Pattullo, Alastair Pearson, Ray Philips, Dawn Powell, Andrew Ramsay, the Reade family, Margaret Rutherford, Karl Simpson, Colin Spencer, Bob Spink, Iain Spink, Ruth Spink, Alan Stuart, Ken Sutherland, the S.W.R.I. and Beverley Tricker.

Thanks also to Maxine Clark for her brilliant food, to Alex, Emma, Saskia, Jim and Katrin at Smith & Gilmour for the design, to Dan Jones for the photography and to Mary Pachnos, my agent. Special thanks to Jo Roberts-Miller and Nicci Praca at Headline for enduring twelve months' pestering with such patience.

And as always I am hugely grateful to my dear family, in particular all the Haddens and Hendersons for memories and recipes; to my parents Bob and Anna Anderson for constant support and photos and stories!; and most of all to Pat, Euan, Faith and Jessica for putting up with my absence on this culinary tour and for helping eat the rewards.

A Puffin in the Porridge

When I read about the St Kildans' tradition of boiling a puffin in with their oats to flavour their porridge, I was fascinated. Having been brought up on porridge cooked with nothing more than oats and salt, I wondered how it might taste and whether or not this curious cooking method had survived after this most westerly and remote of Hebridean islands was evacuated in 1930. All sorts of seabirds were harvested there over the centuries, for their oil, feathers and their flesh. In *An Isle Called Hirte*, author Mary Harman records a visitor to the islands in 1842 enjoying 'a meal consisting of fulmar, auk, guillemot, one of each, boiled; two puffins, roasted; barley cakes, ewe-cheese and milk; and by way of dessert, raw dulse and roasted limpets'. Another visitor in the mid-nineteenth century described the cooking methods: 'puffins were boiled sometimes in the breakfast porridge; and split dried puffins were propped before the fire and roasted'. But I was keen to discover if there was anywhere else in Scotland where such 'delicacies' were still consumed. Was this tradition unique to St Kilda? A trip to the Isle of Lewis where some of the thirty-six St Kildan evacuees ended up, made me aware that puffin consumption did indeed take place elsewhere. Sheriff Colin Scott Mackenzie, Lewis born and bred, told me that in the Lochs area of Lewis, south of Stornoway, it was a delicacy enjoyed by many; indeed he recalls a maid his family employed in the 1940s often enthusing about eating puffin at home. He believes it was still eaten on Lewis as late as the 1960s.

On Tiree, I discovered from fisherman Iain Macdonald that cormorant was a staple of islanders there until the 1970s. And, of course, there is the famous Hebridean delicacy of guga or baby gannet. I met Dods Macfarlane, from Ness on the northern tip of the Isle of Lewis, five years ago to hear about the guga hunting. As part of a legacy that has existed for some four centuries, each summer, he and nine other local men sail to a remote rock in the Atlantic – Sula Sgeir, some 40 miles north of Lewis – to harvest guga. A Statutory Order was inserted into the 1954 Protection of Birds Act that made it illegal to harm gannets, allowing 2,000 to be harvested every year. Once the Nessmen arrive on the tiny island, they set up camp then spend 14 days catching the birds, which involves remarkable skills of rock climbing. Once killed, the birds are decapitated, plucked, singed, dewinged then split. They are then salted and piled in a mound in a wheel formation called a 'pickling stack'. When the men return home to Ness they are met on the quay by locals queuing to buy guga, which are then desalinated, boiled and eaten with potatoes.

And so this year I got a pair, too, and brought them back from Lewis, to savour the rare delicacy in my own home. My fishmonger smoked one and the other I boiled and served with tatties in true Hebridean style. Guga lover Marina Macdonald, brought up on the north of Lewis, told me it is only when she is indulging in her favourite dish of boiled guga and dry tatties that she ever drinks milk. I confess, at my Edinburgh guga dinner, we indulged in drinks more potent than milk – and, in fact, red wine seemed to enhance its unique flavour. Its taste is usually described as fish-meets-fowl, although more fishy (not unlike anchovy) than fowl. Marina, however, thinks it tastes of salty meat and Dods describes it as a mixture of steak and kipper. In the interest of research for this book, not only have I driven, flown and sailed hundreds of miles all over Scotland, mainland and islands, but I have experienced some of the most interesting eating – guga being only one. It was these unique culinary tales and the trail of historic facts that made me consider Scotland's diet, now and then. I was determined to find out more about Scotland's raw ingredients; and so the concept of a culinary tour evolved.

Throughout my tour, I have met fascinating people who produce terrific food, from a beremeal miller in Orkney, a Shetland lamb farmer, the langoustine fishermen of Skye, and a black-pudding maker in Stornoway, to the seaweed collector in Auchmithie and the haddock smoker in Arbroath. They are all wonderful characters, hard working and dedicated. I also had some memorable experiences, from standing, terrified, beside the bee-keeper as he lifted the roof off a hive of angry heather honey bees, to sampling 35 bowls of porridge in the World Porridge-making Championships; and I was momentarily lost for words when a bekilted Highland lady asked me in a cookery demonstration about the possible use of cannabis in my brownies.

The culinary tour is over for this book, but it is certainly not finished. I now realise that, apart from the occasional treat of guga from Lewis, I am unlikely to try many seabirds, certainly not a puffin in my porridge. But what my journey has reinforced, is my conviction that there is so much good food in Scotland – we have the best raw ingredients in the world, from beef, lamb and game to salmon, shellfish, oats and barley. If only we Scots would eschew processed foods and return to our natural, healthy ingredients then, instead of reading the appalling facts about Scottish children being some of the most overweight in the world, we would be celebrating the wonderful and traditional diet enjoyed here for centuries – nutritious oily fish, game, berries, oats and kale. So let's find them, then use them, safe in the knowledge they are healthy and natural. Use them in homely or comforting recipes or in funky, contemporary dishes. But most of all, use them with pride.

Sue on tour (with sister and cousins), Edinburgh, 1960

Lobster,
Langoustines
and Crab

'Imagine Wagner's "Ride of the Valkyries" frozen in stone and hung up like a colossal screen against the sky. It seems as if Nature, when she hurled The Cuillin up into the light of the sun, said, "Their scarred ravines shall lead up to towering spires of rock – unlike any other rock so they will never look the same for very long, now blue, now grey, now silver . . . always drenched in mystery and terrors".' The writer H. V. Morton wrote those words in the 1920s about a visitor's first impression of Skye's Cuillin Hills. And as I stood one balmy evening at Elgol harbour looking beyond the beach and the fishing boats bobbing on the water, at the silhouette of the sun setting behind The Cuillin, I had to agree wholeheartedly. Even seasoned travellers cannot help but feel in awe at the sight of these mountains.

From the pier at Elgol you can look over to the islands of Soay, Canna, Rum and Eigg. There is a daily boat trip on the *Bella Jane* from here, taking you into one of Scotland's most breathtaking lochs, Loch Coruisk, visiting seal colonies en route and enjoying probably the finest views of the Cuillin Hills you will ever see. Or if, like me, hunger overtakes the need for adventure, you can wait on the harbour to see fisherman Colin Lamond come to shore in his boat the *Caella Rose*, bringing in creel upon creel of fabulous langoustines, crabs and squat lobsters. Although most of these are taken immediately by refrigerated van to Broadford then ultimately to Spain, much is still distributed around the island. My hosts for the night, Robin and Lesley Banks at Coruisk House Hotel, manage to negotiate daily with Colin for enough for their guests' dinner. And so a mere 20 minutes after watching the creels unload, I sat in front of a towering platter of freshly boiled seafood with a glass of Muscadet and some home-baked bread, and pondered the word 'fresh' when applied to seafood. Lesley had boiled the langoustines and squat lobster tails for a couple of minutes, the crab claws for ten, then served them warm with home-made mayonnaise. For me, there is no other definition for fresh seafood than dinner at somewhere like Coruisk House, with less than half an hour from boat to plate.

Jim McFarlane has lived in Port Ellen, on the southern tip of the island of Islay his whole life. Now aged 66, and having fished since he was 12, he knows a thing or two about the art. And so, as he explains to me how it has changed over the years, he also shows me his hand-built wooden *sgoth* (Gaelic for skiff), which was the traditional Islay fishing boat for some 200 years, from the mid-eighteenth century.

After the 'golden years', as Jim calls it, from 1975 to 1985, fishing changed on Islay as everywhere else. Sadly nowadays, no one air-dries or salt-cures the saithe or lythe – or the skate wings that were hung up for about a week before being skinned then boiled and eaten almost daily. Nowadays, with lobster stocks depleted, it is crab the Islay fishermen bring in, mainly large brown crabs but also velvet crabs to which the Spaniards are partial. For, as on Skye, the vivier trucks have transported Islay shellfish to France and Spain since the early 1980s. Fortunately, however, things are changing again – this time for the better. More local restaurants are using Islay shellfish, such as the fabulous crab claws and seafood platters served in the Port Charlotte Hotel. Now that tourists can order in restaurants and locals can buy the wonderful Islay crab, lobster and scallops, it seems that, at last, we Scots are appreciating what wonderful produce there is around our shores.

Jim McFarlane's Crab Sandwich

Here is Jim's famous sandwich. To cook his *crubag* he recommends placing it in cold water then slowly bringing it to the boil; this prevents the claws from being cast, which happens if they are plunged directly into boiling water.

SERVES 1

2 slices brown bread, buttered
85–90g/3–3¹/₄ oz crabmeat (half white, half brown)
1 thin slice smoked salmon
a good squeeze of lemon juice
horseradish sauce (optional)

1 Spread one slice of buttered bread with the brown meat then white meat, and then lay the salmon on top.

2 Drizzle the lemon all over and then smear a little horseradish on the other slice of the bread before fixing it on top, cutting and devouring hungrily.

Crab Gratin

This is based on a delicious starter I had in the Hamnavoe Restaurant in Stromness, Orkney. The fabulous Orcadian cheese, Grimbister, with its fresh taste and crumbly texture, is used, but if you cannot find it then substitute with a good farmhouse Wensleydale.

SERVES 3–4

150ml/5 fl oz/¹/₄ pint double cream
100ml/3¹/₂ fl oz dry white wine
100ml/3¹/₂ fl oz chicken stock
450g/1 lb white crab meat
the grated zest of 1 unwaxed lemon
25g/1 oz fresh breadcrumbs
50g/1³/₄ oz Grimbister cheese, grated or finely crumbled
salt and freshly ground black pepper

1 Combine the cream, wine and stock in a pan and bring to the boil. Simmer, uncovered, until reduced to about half the volume; 10 minutes or so. Stir in the crab, heat through, season to taste and stir in the lemon zest.

2 Tip into a gratin dish and top with the breadcrumbs and cheese. Place under a hot grill until the cheese melts. Serve at once with salad and some good bread.

Langoustine and Pea Risotto

An exquisite risotto that needs no introduction – only bowls and forks.

SERVES 4

about 900ml/30 fl oz chicken stock
50g/1³/₄ oz butter
1 small onion, peeled and chopped
300g/10¹/₂ oz risotto rice (arborio or vialone nano)
100ml/3¹/₂ fl oz dry white wine
about 16–20 peeled langoustines (or large prawns, peeled, deveined and cooked)
150g/5¹/₂ oz peas (blanch frozen for 1 minute then drain well; cook fresh until
    just done but still bright green)
the grated zest of 1 large unwaxed lemon
2 tablespoons freshly grated Parmesan cheese
3 or 4 large basil leaves, shredded
salt and freshly ground black pepper

1 Bring the stock to a simmer, and keep simmering.

2 Heat 25g/1 oz of the butter in a large pan, and cook the onion until soft. Add the rice, stir until coated in the fat and beginning to make a slightly crackly sound, then add the wine, and cook until evaporated. Add the hot stock ladle by ladle, stirring continuously, and adding another ladle only once each ladleful been absorbed.

3 Meanwhile, to cook the langoustines, immerse live in boiling water and boil rapidly for 2 minutes. Then plunge into cold water and leave for 3–4 minutes.

4 After cooking the risotto for 15 minutes, add the langoustines or prawns and the peas.

5 You may not need all the stock; it should take 18–20 minutes, or until the rice is *al dente*. Remove the pan from the heat, stir in the lemon zest, then the Parmesan and the remaining butter. Cover and leave to stand for 5 minutes. Finally, stir in the basil and taste for seasoning.

6 To serve, ladle into warm, shallow bowls.

Crab and Rocket Tart

Although Lewis fisherman Dods Macfarlane reckons the best way
to cook crab is on a peat fire (turn once blackened, turn again, crack
open and devour on the beach), not all of us can get the peat.
Fortunately, there is good-quality cooked crab meat available from
fishmongers for us to use in this simple tart, made with only a handful
of ingredients. The combination of crab and rocket with the tang of
crème fraîche and lemon is wonderful.

SERVES 4–6

200g/7 oz plain flour, sifted
125g/4¹/₂ oz unsalted butter, diced
1 large free-range egg, beaten
salt and freshly ground black pepper
FOR THE FILLING
25g/1 oz freshly grated Parmesan cheese
450g/1 lb crabmeat (mainly white meat)
50g/1³/₄ oz rocket
3 large free-range eggs
the grated zest of 1 unwaxed lemon
200ml/7 fl oz/¹/₃ pint crème fraîche

1 For the pastry, place the flour and
butter in a food processor with a pinch
of salt. Process briefly then, with the
machine running, add the egg.
Alternatively, rub in the flour and
butter mixture by hand and stir in the
egg. Bring together with your hands,
and then wrap in clingfilm and chill
for 30 minutes or so.

2 Roll out to fit a deep, 23cm/9 in
tart tin, prick all over and chill well –
preferably overnight. Preheat the
oven to 190°C/375°F/Gas 5. Line
the pastry case with foil and fill with
baking beans, and bake blind for 15
minutes. Remove the foil and cook for

a further 5–10 minutes, or until just
cooked. Remove and sprinkle the
Parmesan cheese for the filling over
the base while still hot. Then cool.

3 Stir the crab and rocket together
(I only chop the rocket if the leaves are
very large) then add the eggs, lemon
zest and crème fraîche, seasoning
with plenty of salt and pepper (taste
it if you can bear to, to ensure you
have just enough seasoning, adding
more salt and pepper if necessary).
Pour into the pastry case and bake
for 40–45 minutes, or until set and
tinged with golden brown. Serve
warm or cold with salad.

Tiree Seafood Salad

Jane Macdonald, who lives on a croft in the hamlet of Ruaig on the
Hebridean island of Tiree, has the most amazing array of salad leaves
in her polytunnels; from ruby chard and winter purslane to endive
and spinach, she grows these to sell to a café in the village of Baugh
and at the Farmers' Market on the island. Jane is married to islander
Iain, who was a fisherman specialising in scallops, lobsters and crabs,
but now takes visitors on boat trips to Fingal's Cave on the island of
Staffa – or to nearby Coll – via the dolphin and seal colonies.

Jane makes this delicious salad whenever they have a lobster or
crab to cook. She garnishes it with the crab or lobster claws, which
not only makes it look good but it also ekes out the eating time from
a possible half hour to three. She advises boiling crab and lobster
in a gently rolling boil, never fierce, for fear that the gloriously
tender meat will become overcooked.

None of this can possibly be as memorable as what Iain was
brought up on: the Tiree staple – cormorant – which was boiled then
fried and served with tatties, before it became a protected bird a
couple of decades ago. Its taste, according to Iain, was between fish
and liver. I think I'll stick with this salad, however, which tastes,
quite simply, delicious.

SERVES 3–4

about 200g/7 oz mixed salad leaves, such as rocket, lettuce, land cress,
    purslane, mizuna and lambs lettuce
the juice of 1 lemon
2 teaspoons pesto
1 teaspoon honey
3 tablespoons extra virgin olive oil
400–500g/14 oz–1 lb 2 oz freshly boiled crab (picked; white meat only)
    or lobster, (diced)
salt and freshly ground black pepper

1 Place the salad in a large bowl.
Combine the lemon juice, pesto,
honey and olive oil in a small bowl,
seasoning to taste.

2 Pour this over the salad, top with
the crab or lobster and toss gently
together. Serve with good bread.

Mussels, Oysters and Scallops

Just like in so many other coastal places around Britain, mussels have been collected along the shore of the Dornoch Forth for centuries. But in this most northerly of Scotland's Firths, the Crown gave up its rights to the mussels 6 miles from the shore almost 400 years ago, making it unique in Britain. So, since 1612 when James VI (James I of England) bequeathed the ownership of the mussel 'scalps' (rocky outcrops) to the Royal Burgh of Tain in perpetuity, the locals have been legally permitted to harvest the wild mussels. The Tain Mussel Fishery now forms part of the Common Good Fund of the old Royal Burgh area, this fund helping finance local community projects. The company, Highland Mussels Ltd, now harvests the wild mussels, which are usually gathered when around 4–5 years old, much older than their farmed cousins. Even older wild mussels are left as brood stock. The wild mussels, apart from being sandier than farmed, also have heavier shells and are generally smaller. The French market love them and so hundreds of tonnes are exported to Brittany to be served in their mussel, garlic and white wine dishes.

Even further north, I went to see Demlane Mussels, now one of Scotland's largest suppliers of rope-grown (farmed) mussels, begun in 1995 by Joy and Jim Tait in Walls on the west of Shetland's mainland. When they began, although they knew the potential for a premium product was there because the wild ones were so good, they were taking an enormous risk as, unlike salmon farming where you start with eggs that become fry and eventually salmon, with mussels there is nothing to see. Mussel farming begins as a complete mystery. At the start of the mussel-growing season all that can be seen are tiny dots, rather like a Pointillist painting, then, according to Shetlander Jim Tait with tongue firmly in his cheek, 'the rest is in God's hands'.

To understand what he meant I was taken to one of their seven sites, in some of the cleanest, most unpolluted waters in the world. Just before the spawning season in March and April, 8-metre-long ropes are dropped down from a 'header rope' about 200 metres long. Billions of spawn float freely for the first four to six weeks, before growing their 'beards' which mean they can attach themselves to something: in the wild, a rock; on a mussel farm, the rope. And that is all there is to it. Unlike other types of aquaculture, there is no daily feeding or cosseting; once the microscopic larvae have attached, they grow naturally, feeding on plankton. But it is not all plain sailing: there is the ever-present danger of eider ducks swooping down to steal the mussels. And it is a long wait; only after 2½–3 years are the mussels the right size to harvest.

The water depth, tidal flow and shelter are optimum in these Shetland 'voes' (small fjords). Water depth is important as the ropes must not touch the seabed or starfish will climb up and feast! The tidal flow and shelter are crucial. The water needs to be clean and unpolluted with just enough ebb and flow to ensure water purity, but not so much that the mussels are unable to cling on to the ropes and are carried away by the tide.

And so, what do we get from all this? Mussels are very healthy: low in fat and cholesterol, they are high in omega-3 fatty acids. As for the taste – fabulous.

It was touch and go whether I'd even make it to the Islay Oyster Farm. I took the first, instead of the second, single-track road and was soon up at the top of the hill, beyond the cattle grid. I looked down over the brow of the hill and there, a mere 15 metres away, in the middle of my path, was the largest bull I have ever seen. The size of a small elephant, it was not only not for budging, it started to look at my little red (yes, red) car with more than passing interest. I slowly put the car into reverse and drove down the road faster than I – or possibly anyone – have ever reversed. When I arrived at Islay Oysters, the owner, Craig Archibald, who also farms Aberdeen Angus cross cattle, asked me what colour the bull was. When I said fawn, he said, 'Ah well, that's all right then; not one of mine.' I presumed he meant that only black bulls might have charged me. No, actually, he was worried I might have upset one of his own prize Angus bulls.

Craig and father Tony began farming oysters as a sideline to their cattle, sheep, barley and oats, on the shores of Loch Gruinart on the island of Islay, in 1988. The spats, aged about 3–6 months, arrive from Barrow-in-Furness and grow until they are about 2 years old. They have been described in print and verbally all over the island as 'the greatest oysters in the Northern hemisphere'; they are indeed almost uniquely plump and juicy. The reason why is because the two 'must-haves' for oyster cultivation are an abundant supply of clear water and plankton. Loch Gruinart has both. They farm the Pacific oyster, which can be eaten all year, unlike the native European oysters, which breed during the summer months. And it is not only the year-round availability that makes them so sought after but it is also their consistent quality. And they have the Gulf Stream to warm the water in winter and the average Scottish weather which means temperatures never rise too much, so the water remains more or less the same temperature, which is ideal for oysters. Because Loch Gruinart is an estuary, it is tidal and so the oysters spend their lives filtering the nutrient-rich seawater, which is changed twice a day by the tide. Like all oysters they are low in fat and high in vitamins and minerals, zinc in particular.

Just like the excellent Islay lamb, beef and pork as well as other shellfish, more oysters are being sold locally to Islay chefs. They cook them or more often serve them raw with nothing more than chilled white wine, although the local Finlaggan Ale is also proffered with a plate of oysters at the Port Charlotte Hotel. The other obvious choice is whisky, given the eight world-famous distilleries on this small Hebridean island. Many people (but never locals: sacrilege!) drizzle their Islay oysters with some malt whisky, the best match being the less peaty ones such as Bunnahabhain or Bruichladdich. Tony likes to toss freshly opened oysters into an omelette or remove the lid and grill with a splash of cream and some grated cheese.

But both Tony and Craig tell me what is crucial about serving oysters: open them, tip away any salt water and then leave them for one minute so that the natural juices come out. Craig also tells me that it is 'rubbish' that you must only swallow and never chew oysters. Certainly for first-timers, chewing makes the oysters less of a challenge.

On the remote Isle of Ewe in Wester Ross, the phrase 'doing the school run' takes on a totally different meaning. Jane Grant lines up the island's five school-age children on the beach at 7.30 a.m. Monday to Friday. They then all don wellies, oilskins and life jackets over their school uniform, and she helps them clamber into a small motor boat in the shallow water. They then transfer to a well-equipped 28-footer which she motors just over a mile across the stunningly beautiful Loch Ewe to Aultbea where the primary children go to school and the secondary ones catch the school bus to Gairloch. On fine summer mornings, nothing could be nicer, but in the middle of winter when it is cold, wet – and pitch black – it is a different story. And once Jane has done the morning run, there is no popping back home to put her feet up with a coffee until the afternoon run. There is the post to collect for delivery back on the island, potential calls from Nato – and starfish to annihilate. For Jane Grant's chief job – apart from doing the school run, helping moor frigates for Nato, acting as post-mistress for the 12 island residents and looking after crofter husband Willie and sons Philip and Steven – is scallop farmer. And, apart from the midges, starfish are Jane's enemy number one, for if even one tiny starfish is left in with a batch of 500 baby scallops, at the end of the winter there will be one extremely large starfish and not a single scallop: an expensive oversight indeed.

But let me go back to the beginning of the cycle of scallop farming to show where eliminating the predators comes in. Jane Grant was quick to point out that her method of aquaculture is not classic textbook, but then unless there is a book written on the sea, winds, sun and rain on her own 'Several Order' (the piece of seabed, about 400 x 150 metres that only she is allowed to use for scallops), she has to make it up as she goes along. Before you have scallops, you need spat (juvenile bivalves), which she collects in September in the Summer Isles, a short journey north. (During May and June when scallops reproduce, eggs float in the plankton and begin to settle on seaweed in the wild; Jane replicates this with spat bags filled with mono-filament hung on weighted lines some 40 metres deep.) These spat bags are then hauled up and brought back to Loch Ewe to grow slowly into the shellfish we know and love.

During the next – rather tedious – stage, Jane involves the children. It is now late September or October and time to sort out the spat, which are about 5mm in size. The net bags contain not only these tiny little scallops but also crab, sea urchins and the dreaded starfish. Jane admits this sorting procedure is the worst part of scallop farming, not only because she has to confront enemy number one but it is also a filthy job, as the bags are covered with seaweed and jellyfish. Once every vestige of other sea creatures has been removed, the tiny scallops are set in plastic oyster trays and hung about 10 metres down from buoys to overwinter. Because the water is so cold during the winter they do not actually grow, but hibernate in their safe trays, far away from the stormy surface waters – and tightly enclosed against predators.

Come June, they are moved from the trays into 'lantern nets', which allow more room for growth. These nets are also hung from buoys, safe and calm, for Jane insists a healthy scallop is all down to good husbandry and protection from predators until they are big enough to go solo on the seabed. Ideal conditions are those in Loch Ewe with its shallow waters and good tidal flow; they also seem to like the peace and quiet of the seabed. These tranquil molluscs remain snugly in the lantern nets until the following April when they are removed and thrown on to the seabed. And it is here, under the sea, they remain until fully grown, which takes anything from 2–3 years. After two years down under, they will be about 11cm (medium size); she also sells large scallops that are up to 13–14cm. They are brought up by a team of three divers at harvest time, which is usually before Christmas, then those scallops not being sold immediately are held in 'keep bags', ready to be collected as orders come in.

And, slowly, local hotels are increasing their orders. One customer is Alastair Pearson, proprietor at the charming Old Inn in Gairloch. When he took over the hotel in 1999 there was a preponderance of frozen scampi and chicken nuggets. Now he uses local produce such as haddock dipped in their own real-ale batter, wild venison and Jane Grant's scallops, served in myriad ways, one of the most unusual involving drying the scallop roe and grinding it into powder as a garnish. If more Scottish hoteliers followed Alastair's lead and eschewed frozen processed foods, perhaps we would be universally proud of our food. And all thanks to people like Jane Grant who is committed to improving quality local produce . . . while juggling school runs, Nato work, postal duties and crofting. The term superwoman might have been born in Hollywood but the real thing lives on a scallop farm in Wester Ross.

Oysters in Oatmeal

For those oyster virgins who think they'll hate them – simply because
they are told they have to swallow them raw and pulsating – this one's
for them. They are very quickly and gently cooked until still soft
and almost creamy in texture – exquisite!

SERVES 2–3
12 oysters
about 60g/2¼ oz medium oatmeal
25g/1 oz butter
the juice of 1 lemon

1 To shuck the oysters: wrap your
left hand in a tea towel (assuming
you are right handed) and place an
oyster, cup-side down, hinge towards
you, in your palm. Insert an oyster
knife or small, sharp knife into the
hinge. Push and twist simultaneously,
passing the knife under the top shell
to cut the muscle and sliding it along
the length to open fully. Remove the
oyster from the shell.

2 Dip into oatmeal and chill briefly.
Heat the butter in a frying pan then
gently fry the oysters, turning once,
for 1–1½ minutes altogether (no
more). Squeeze with lemon juice
and eat at once.

Spaghetti with Mussels

This dish, inspired by Sicilian recipes for seafood spaghetti (often using anchovies or sardines) might seem incongruous in a Scottish food book. But when my father showed me a picture of his father, my Grandad Anderson, sitting chatting (in which language?) with locals in a bar in Messina, Sicily, in 1926 as if he was one of the natives, I realised that perhaps mince and tatties was not the only food known to my Dundee ancestors. As Chief Engineer in the Merchant Navy, he had certainly been around, and I like to think that on his trips to Italy he introduced his Dundonian palate to the joys of pasta.

SERVES 2

500–600g/1 lb 2 oz–1 lb 5 oz mussels, well scrubbed and beards pulled off
4 tablespoons extra virgin olive oil
1 small fennel bulb, trimmed and chopped
100ml/3¹/₂ fl oz dry white wine
3 garlic cloves, peeled and chopped
¹/₂–1 red chilli (amount depends on your heat tolerance), finely chopped
400g/14 oz tin chopped tomatoes
2 tablespoons capers
200g/7 oz spaghetti or linguini

1 Discard any mussels that do not close when sharply tapped. Heat 2 tablespoons of the oil in a large pan and add the fennel. Cook for 4–5 minutes then add the mussels and white wine. Cover the pan and shake well, then cook for 2–3 minutes, just until they open. (Discard any that remain closed.)

2 Pour through a colander over a bowl, reserving both solids and liquids. Once cool enough to handle, remove most of the mussels from their shells and discard the shells. Set the mussels aside.

3 Heat the remaining oil in a pan and fry the garlic and chilli for 30 seconds, then add the tomatoes, capers and the reserved liquor from the mussels. Stir, then bubble away for 5 minutes or so, stirring until reduced a little.

4 Meanwhile, cook the pasta until al dente, and drain.

5 Tip the shelled mussels and fennel into the tomato sauce, stir well then tip this into the pasta, tossing well. Top with the whole unshelled mussels and serve in warm bowls.

Grandad Anderson (far left) in Messina, Sicily, 1926

Oysters with Sausages

This combination might sound bizarre, but it is one of the nicest: the ice-cold oyster with the mouth-janglingly hot sausage. I prefer it made with beef sausages, but pork are also good.

SERVES SEVERAL, AS CANAPÉS
500g/1 lb 2 oz good beef sausages (with high meat content), halved
16–20 oysters

1 Grill the sausages until cooked through and place on a dish.

2 Meanwhile, open the oysters (see page 21). Tip away the sea water. Discard the rounded shell. Remove the oyster from the flat shell. Place the oysters in their half-shells on ice alongside the sausages. Eat hot sausage then cold oyster.

Barra Scallops with Cockles

Flying to Barra and landing on the beach had always been a dream of mine. Landing in gale force 9 winds was not. However, after a few scary minutes, circling over the wild, angry seas, we landed at Eoligary on the north-east of Barra in the Outer Hebrides. The airfield, with its three runways 'sketched' out in the sand, is a huge tidal beach called Cockle Strand. At the Barra Heritage Centre there are old black-and-white pictures of locals collecting large bags of cockles, now mainly for export, on this beach at the end of the runway. In 1549, High Dean of The Isles, Donald Munro, wrote of Barra: 'into the sandis growis great Cockles . . . thair is not ane fairer and mair profitable sandis for Cockles in ony pairt of the world.' Locals still collect them for themselves (traditionally just boiled or eaten raw); but at the Isle of Barra Hotel they serve them with garlic butter.

That night, after my interesting touchdown on Barra, I relaxed over dinner at the Isle of Barra Hotel with a dish of the largest scallops I have ever seen (local of course), cooked simply in dill butter. The recipe here is my tribute to one of the most thrilling journeys ever, to one of the most stunning Scottish islands and to the island's outstanding scallops.

SERVES 2
6 plump scallops
extra virgin olive oil
25g/1 oz butter
150g/5½ oz cockles (shelled weight), cooked
2 tablespoons chopped fresh dill

1 Rub the scallops in a little oil then heat a frying pan to very hot, add a smear of oil then add the scallops. Fry them for 2 minutes, turning after 1 minute or so, then remove them to a warm plate.

2 Add the butter to the pan then add the cockles and heat until hot. Add the dill, toss everything together, tip on top of the scallops and serve at once with good bread, as a starter (or serve as a main course, with roasted vegetables).

Roast Beef with Oyster Sauce

Most traditional oyster sauce recipes with roast beef are flour-based or enriched with cream to make rich, excessively indulgent sauces. Mine is ludicrously simple and yet rather effective, as the texture and flavour of the oysters remain good.

SERVES 3-4

small joint of beef rib roast
12 oysters
40g/1½ oz butter
the juice of 1 large lemon
salt and freshly ground black pepper

1 Preheat the oven to 230°C/450°F/ Gas 8. Ensure the beef is at room temperature by removing it from the fridge at least an hour before cooking. Place in a roasting tin, season all over then place in the oven, without any extra fat, for 15 minutes. Reduce the heat to 170°C/325°F/Gas 3 and continuing to roast for 17 minutes per 500g/1lb 2 oz (this will give you medium-rare). Once it is cooked to your liking, remove the beef carefully to a carving board. Rest the beef, loosely covered in foil, for at least 20 minutes.

2 About 10 minutes before carving, open the oysters (see page 21). Tip away the salt water. Remove the oyster from the flat shell. Leave for a minute to allow the natural juices to come out then tip the liquor into a bowl and keep the oysters separate.

3 Heat the butter in a pan and, once hot, add the oysters. Cook for no more than half a minute altogether, turning once, then remove them with a slotted spoon. Keep warm. Add the oyster liquor to the pan and bubble away for a minute or so, then add the lemon juice and season to taste with pepper. (You will probably not need salt.) Return the oysters to the pan, tip it all into a small serving dish and serve with the beef.

Scallops with Black Pudding on Champit' Peas

The combination of scallops and black pudding is one made in heaven. And, combined with these mashed, or champit', peas, it becomes even more fabulous!

SERVES 3-4

300g/10½ oz peas (fresh or frozen)
400g/14 oz tin of butter beans, drained
the juice of 1 large lemon
1 heaped teaspoon ground cumin
1 garlic clove, peeled
about 7 tablespoons extra virgin olive oil
3–4 slices black pudding
9–12 scallops
salt and freshly ground black pepper

1 For the peas, cook until just done then drain and run under a cold tap to arrest cooking and retain their bright green colour. Pat thoroughly dry on kitchen paper then tip into a food processor with the butter beans, lemon juice, cumin and garlic. Whiz briefly then add enough olive oil, about 5 tablespoons, to form a thickish purée. Season to taste and set aside.

2 Heat 2 tablespoons oil in a frying pan then, once hot, add the black pudding and fry until crispy, a couple of minutes each side. Remove and transfer to a warm plate. Increase the heat and add the scallops. Fry for 1–2 minutes on each side, depending on the thickness.

3 To serve, place a dollop of the champit' peas (warm or at room temperature) on warm plates and top with a slice of black pudding and then the scallops.

Salmon

Karl Scott lifts a scoop of feed and flings it over the large pen of water with the dexterity of years of experience. As the sun glints on the crystal-clear water, I screw up my eyes against the glare of the sunshine and wait. Then up they leap, back-flipping and somersaulting more deftly than Olympic gymnasts. This is Shetland and these are the salmon.

Well, technically, they are not in fact salmon but smolts. In the wild, smolt is the name of the salmon at the time they transfer from fresh to salt water (before this they are called parr; and fry before that). There are more technical terms: a grilse is a smaller salmon that has spent one winter at sea; only after more than one winter can we call this king of fish a salmon. And as I talk to Karl Scott, whose father, Jim Scott, was the first Shetland salmon farmer back in 1982, I find out about how the life of a farmed salmon copies the life of its wild counterpart, the Atlantic salmon, *Salmo salar*.

For farmed salmon, brood stock are stripped of eggs, then the eggs are kept in tanks until they become fry at 3–4 months old. At this point, they are removed to larger tanks and at about 1 year old are known as smolts. The smolts are taken to pens in the sea when they are between 75g and 100g where they live for 1^{1}/$_{2}$–2 years before being harvested at around 5kg. The farm sites are then left fallow for a period of several months per cycle before being restocked, just as good husbandry onshore dictates.

To my mind, it is impossible to comment on the welfare of farmed salmon unless one has visited a salmon farm. The one I visited in the sea west of Shetland was testament to the fact that the situation and the method of farming are crucial. Here (where, as well as in Orkney, lower stocking densities exist), with the fast-running currents of the north Atlantic, there is natural ebb and flow of ocean-driven water (rare in some inshore sea lochs). This causes the fish to swim vigorously – and in some of the most unpolluted water in the world. In the voes (Shetland's small fjords) there is very little fresh-water run-off, since there are no rivers in Shetland, and so the chances of farmed salmon escaping into the rivers, as has happened elsewhere, is impossible.

As we stand on the edge of the pen of water some 50m deep, a smaller fishing boat passes (the owners fishing are for velvet crabs and 'buckies', Karl tells me) and, after a brief greeting, the still silence returns as Karl continues to feed the fish. They are fed four times a day at this stage ('It's like feeding a baby – little and often,' he says) and always by hand. Then, once the fish get to a certain size they are fed via a pipe on the boat. When they near harvest time at about 20–22 months, they are fed twice and then once a day, with underwater cameras being lowered into the pen to check on the feeding. The minute the fish stop eating, the pipe feed stops supplying the food. This, therefore, counteracts the criticism of waste food contamination on the seabed. And as for antibiotics, Karl cannot remember the last time they were used; perhaps some 15 years ago. With good husbandry, it is usually unnecessary.

And if anyone is still anxious about the 'cruelty' involved in salmon farming, they simply need to select their salmon wisely. Shetland salmon, with its unique natural environment producing firm-textured fish, which, of course, is packed full of omega-3 fatty acids is an obvious choice. One visit to Shetland with its good tidal flow, unpolluted water and low stocking density should help convince the discerning customer. The conditions where the fish are reared are as close to raw nature as you'll get. If still in doubt, however, bear in mind that salmon naturally shoal in close proximity. And anyone who has witnessed battery chickens rammed together either in barns without any provision to the outdoors or, even worse, the egg-layers who are stuck in cages without a proper floor and with simply wire for their claws, will confirm that, by comparison, salmon kept in pens such as those I witnessed have room to do what comes naturally: in their case, swim – and swim fast. It also seems to me that not only is there nothing to hide on Shetland farms but, indeed, there is much to be proud of. And as for the taste: Shetland salmon is not called the *grand cru* of salmon for nothing.

Back at home, I visited my Edinburgh fishmonger, Gaven Borthwick at Armstrong's of Stockbridge to see what becomes of some of this catch. He cold-smokes salmon all year: pin-boning a whole side, he rubs fine salt all over before smoking, leaving it for 10 to 12 hours. It is then rinsed off and soaked in fresh water for 20 minutes and finally left on racks to dry thoroughly for at least 10 hours. Then, the shop's own traditional marinade is rubbed in by hand and the side is smoked over oak chips for a minimum of two nights and a maximum of three days: the drier it becomes, the easier it is to slice. Gaven also smokes sides of wild salmon, both in season and from frozen during the festive season. Smoked wild salmon has a firmer, drier texture and the taste is slightly more gamey, without any oily residue on the palate. But, at double the price, it is most certainly a treat. With the protection of wild stocks uppermost in responsible consumers' minds, it is interesting to learn that the 'Catch and Release' policy as a successful management tool is on the increase throughout the country. Let's hope this brings a slow reversal in the decline of the annual catch of wild salmon. Then, perhaps, we won't have to save it only for special occasions.

Sue and big sister Carol at Loch Feochan near Oban, 1963

Frittata with Smoked Salmon

While on Shetland, I visited Dave and Debbie Hammond who ran the Shetland Smokehouse for 15 years. They began smoking sides of salmon at their home in the village of Skeld in the early 1980s and sold both these and smoked haddock door to door. Some 25 years on, they built up a small factory producing a range of fabulous fish pâtés, marinated herring, gravadlax and, of course, cold- and hot-smoked salmon, which is smoked over old whisky barrels.

This is Dave's recipe for a slow-cooked, rich omelette made with various flavourings, then topped with smoked salmon and grilled lightly. Usually done with thinly sliced cold-smoked salmon, it is also good with flakes of hot-smoked.

SERVES 2–3
6 large free-range eggs
200ml/7 fl oz/^{1}/₃ pint crème fraîche
2 teaspoons horseradish sauce
^{1}/₂ small red onion, peeled and finely chopped
10g/^{1}/₄ oz chives, chopped
25g/1 oz butter
100g/3^1/₂ oz thinly sliced smoked salmon
the juice of 1 lime or lemon
salt and freshly ground black pepper

1 Beat the eggs and crème fraîche with the horseradish and a little seasoning. Lightly sauté the onion and chives in the butter until just softened then, over a medium heat, tip in the egg mixture. Leave for a couple of minutes then, with a spatula, push in from the sides. Cook for 7–8 minutes, or until almost set.

2 Lay the smoked salmon slices over. Place under a preheated hot grill for 2–3 minutes, or until the eggs are just set, then squeeze over the lemon juice and serve at once in wedges, with salad.

Smoked Salmon Pâté

Nowadays smoked salmon pâté is almost a cliché, but this recipe is so quick, so easy and so utterly delicious, I defy you to not make this a regular weekly dish.

SERVES 6

125g/4½ oz smoked salmon (trimmings are fine but are often saltier)
125g/4½ oz light cream cheese
the grated zest and juice of 1 unwaxed lemon
freshly ground black pepper

1 Whiz everything together in a food processor until creamy. Season to taste with pepper (you will probably not need salt).

2 Remove to a serving dish and chill for a couple of hours before serving with toast. You could also spread the pâté on to slices of thin crustless brown bread then cut them up and make into little rolls, as canapés.

Hot-smoked Salmon Pancakes

This recipe is based on a wonderful starter that was cooked by Chef Kareen Horne at the Waterside Hotel in Peterhead. She presented three dainty little salmon pancakes on a plate with a seared scallop on each and a drizzle of sweet-and-sour red pepper dressing. This makes a delicious starter, combined with scallops, but I also like the pancakes just as they are, served warm, as canapés. But do provide napkins.

SERVES MANY, AS CANAPÉS

about 300g/10½ oz potatoes, peeled
25g/1 oz plain flour
1 large free-range egg
150g/5½ oz hot-smoked salmon, flaked
1 heaped tablespoon dill, chopped
about 1 tablespoon milk
butter, for greasing
salt and freshly ground black pepper

1 Boil the potatoes in unsalted water then drain well and mash. Cool to just warm then add the remaining ingredients with enough milk to form a thickish mixture. Season to taste with salt and pepper.

2 Heat a girdle (griddle) or heavy frying pan to hot then smear with butter. Once hot, drop teaspoonfuls of the mixture on to the surface and cook for about 3 minutes altogether, turning after 1–2 minutes. They are ready when they are golden brown on both sides but still slightly squishy in the middle.

3 Eat warm (or allow to cool, then reheat in a medium oven).

Fresh Salmon Chowder

An old pub five minutes from my house is mentioned in the book *Old Edinburgh Taverns* as having been erected in 1821 as a landing-stage for steam-packets. Nowadays, the Old Chain Pier serves good food, particularly local seafood. A favourite of mine is Trinity Chowder. Here is my version – based on a Finnish salmon soup recipe.

SERVES 3–4
400g/14 oz potatoes (peeled weight), peeled and diced
700ml/1¼ pints fish (or light chicken) stock
1 large leek, cleaned, thinly sliced
8–10 black peppercorns
300g/10½ oz fresh salmon, skinned (tail-end fillet is fine)
200ml/7 fl oz/⅓ pint double cream
20g/¾ oz fresh chives, snipped
salt

1 Place the potatoes and stock in a saucepan, and bring to the boil. Cook for about 10 minutes, or until the potatoes are almost, but not quite, tender. Add the leek and peppercorns (no salt yet). Stir.

2 Cut the salmon into large chunks and place these on top. Cover and simmer for about 10 minutes over a low heat until the fish is just cooked. Add salt to taste then gently stir in the cream, taking great care not to break up the fish. Reheat for a minute or so then stir in the chives. Taste again to check the seasoning then serve in warm bowls.

Haddock
and Herring

Iain Spink replaces the tarry poke over the barrel, then emerges, eyes streaming, from a great billowing cloud of smoke. He has in his hand a smokie, straight off the barrel. He opens it up, slips out the bone and offers me some. The moist warm flesh tastes divine. It is the most delicious smokie ever; one of the best fish I have ever tasted.

And the long queue forming at Cupar Farmers' Market bears testimony to the fact that I am not alone in my opinion. They have been placing their orders since 8.00 a.m., ready to return at 9.00 a.m. when Iain has the first batch ready. Iain, scion of the Arbroath smokie Spink family, has given craft demonstrations for over a year now, keen to revive the traditional curing method that originated in Auchmithie and then was taken to Arbroath during the nineteenth century.

The history of the smokie is fascinating and has been sketched out for me by Bob Spink, Iain's father. Auchmithie itself was more than likely a Viking settlement and, although the first official mention of the village is 1434, it is believed that there has been a village on that site from AD1000. A quick visit north to the Shetlands, where the Viking link is indisputable since it was as 'recently' as 1468 that both Shetland and Orkney were pledged to Scotland as part of the marriage dowry of Margaret, princess of Norway, on her marriage to James of Scotland (later James III), strengthens the Viking theory since fish ('sillocks', members of the saithe family) are smoked there in exactly the same manner as the Arbroath smokies. Back in Auchmithie this unique smoking method was also used on other fish beside the haddock – herring, dabs, cod – just like in Shetland. From 1830 on, several Auchmithie families agreed to move to Arbroath, taking with them, of course, their fishing skills and, more importantly (for us), their fish-curing know-how.

The fishwives of Auchmithie – and later Arbroath – wore a particular outfit of several skirts or petticoats (called coats) of coarse navy-blue flannel, the outer layers folded up and tucked up to support the willow creel in which they carried their merchandise to market; it was kept in position by a broad band that went over their head and crossed the chest. They also wore a fancy blouse, often with mother of pearl buttons, a striped cotton pleated apron and a plaid or checked shawl crossed over at the front. My parents remember the Arbroath and Auchmithie fishwives coming to their home town of Dundee to sell fish from their creels. The fishwives would climb up and down the stone tenement stairs ringing at every door.

My brother-in-law's grandmother, Isabella (Ise) Smith, was one of Arbroath's last fishwives to go far afield to sell the fish – mainly smokies but also Finnan haddie. Once a week, she travelled all the way from Arbroath to Perth and Almondbank (in Perthshire) to sell fish to the 'big houses' there. She was away for the entire day, most of which was spent travelling by train to Perth then onwards by bus. Amazingly, she continued this until she was nearly 70 years old, which was in the late 1960s.

But back to Iain Spink: he attends Cupar Farmers' Market and any fairs where he can dig his halved whisky barrel into the ground to make his fire with oak or beech wood. The adage 'No smoke without fire' was never truer than in the preparation of the famous smokie. The day before, Iain beheads and cleans the gutted whole haddock, then ties them in pairs and dry salts them for anything from 1½ to 5 hours, depending on size and firmness. The salt is then washed off in fresh water and then they are left to hang to dry the skins out. Ideally this would be done overnight, but 20 minutes at a smoke-encompassed stall at the Farmers' Market does the job just as well.

The poles the fish are hung over are made of wood traditionally; commercial producers have to use stainless steel nowadays because of EC legislation. Because Iain is giving a craft demonstration, however, he can still use wood. Whether or not Iain's superb fish can be called Arbroath smokies is a moot point, though, since these have recently joined the ranks of Stilton, Parma ham and champagne – awarded Protected Geographical Indication (PGI) status by the EC, which means it must be produced in the traditional manner within a 5-mile radius of Arbroath. This is not only a boost to the smaller cottage industries in and around Arbroath, but also means that so-called Arbroath smokies from London or Hull are no longer entitled to use the name. It is ironic that it is Iain's father, Bob Spink, whose family has produced smokies in the town for five generations, who has fronted the campaign to achieve this status. However, because Iain's is a traditional display rather than a commercial enterprise, his smokies can be called 'Original Smokies from Arbroath' by rights; the customers in the queue simply call them 'delicious'.

After the poles are laid on the barrels, they are covered with the 'tarry poke' (Auchmithie's smokie doyenne, Margaret Horn's terminology for the cover), or as Iain calls it, a smokie cloot. They are left for 40 minutes or so, turning once halfway through. Then they are removed from the barrel, all golden and tarry, dripping with tasty, salty juices, ready to be taken home for tea or eaten there and then straight from the paper. I can think of no better nor more natural Scottish fast food.

And from son Iain to father Bob I see the traditional and the modern. On a visit to R.R. Spink's brand new factory in Arbroath, I saw the smokie (produced within the city's 5-mile boundaries and therefore a genuine Arbroath smokie) being made in the modern way. Once gutted, it is still beheaded, washed and tied in pairs by hand. The fish are dry-salted then rinsed, hung on trolleys with stainless steel poles (no wooden poles for anyone supplying supermarkets) then they are smoked over a beech and oak wood fire for some 30 minutes. There is of course no 'tarry poke' but a stainless steel 'box' device instead. It might not look as charming as Iain's traditional method but they still taste pretty good. Although, as both father and son avow, there is absolutely nothing to beat the taste of a smokie straight off the wooden pole and the wooden barrel. Warm and moist, it is a taste of the sea; it is also a taste of the past that is now very much part of the twenty-first century.

When my parents and aunts started to tell me about the Dundee tradition they remembered of giving dressed herring as a good luck symbol at New Year, I assumed this was a 'dressed' (in breadcrumbs?) fish, presumably already cooked. How wrong could I be! The quaint tradition, which originated in fact in Arbroath, actually involved cured herrings being dressed in hats and dresses, made of brightly coloured crêpe paper, with ribbons, bows and fringes. Their little wizened heads poke out of the top to resemble wistful old spinsters trying to regain their piscine youth. A very strange custom indeed.

Arbroath fish expert Robert Spink persuaded his sister Ruth to dress three beautiful herrings that Robert had dry-salted for seven days, hung on tenterhooks for a day then heavily smoked for three days – especially for me. The tradition of giving a dressed herring continued until the early 1960s in Arbroath; in Dundee it had died out some years before that. The dressed and bonneted herrings (now stiff from the curing) were hung on the inside of the front door for the entire year to bring luck. It is hardly surprising that the tradition arrived in Dundee, whence my relatives remember it, since the Arbroath fisherwives sold their wares in Dundee daily and would have brought them along for the New Year tradition, along with their smokies and fresh fish.

According to Robert, the 'dressed herring' spoken of now were never known as such; they were always referred to as 'red herring', so the proper term would be 'dressed red herring'. Why and where they became 'dressed' and why this tradition took on in coastal Angus, no one seems to know. Probably in fisher households where poverty was the norm, the wish that next year would bring good catches of herring led to enhancing what was easy for them to come by as a good luck token, rather like corn dollies on haystacks.

Red herring themselves have been exported from Britain since the seventeenth century, and probably much before that. Some say the east coast fishing communities were eating them 700 years ago. Red herring was described by Thomas Nash in 1567 as 'a bloater more strongly cured'.

Like the more common salt herring in barrels, huge amounts of these red herring were exported to the West Indies, where they were deemed suitable high-protein food for the enslaved population. Herring that were landed at Arbroath and nearby ports were shipped out of Montrose, not only to the West Indies but also to the Baltic ports. The method for curing red herring – the longest smoked and the strongest-tasting herring – is quoted by Nash as 'Roused in brine for up to 3 weeks, they were then hung high up in the smokehouse for up to another 3 weeks, hence they were also known as "high-dries".'

The other old-fashioned methods of curing herring – salting or sousing (potting) – are seen less frequently nowadays, but up in Orkney there is a roaring trade in marinating herring. Founded in 1987, The Orkney Herring Company now sells their marinated herring all over the UK following a recent promotion of the health-giving properties of the fish. In G.W. Lockhart's *The Scots and their Fish*, the author declares, 'The food value of herring is well known. The herring is more nourishing and contains more necessary vitamins and minerals than any other fish, flesh or fowl.' And indeed the health benefits of omega-3, whose richest source is oil-rich fish such as herring, mackerel, sardines, and so on, are well publicised. As well as benefits to joints and skin, it is also known to help arthritis and eczema, but it is perhaps most often associated with healthy heart maintenance. So much so that an Orkney doctor, Dr Andrew Trevett, made headlines in 2000 when he prescribed herring to his patients with existing heart problems.

Up at The Orkney Herring Company in Stromness, the ancient fishing port and formerly one of Orkney's herring stations, they are making a huge range of different marinades to tempt consumers back to this super-healthy fish. And since so many fussy eaters are put off by the bones in herring, their product is ideal because through either sousing (potting) – which involves cooking the fish – or marinating in vinegar or acetic acid, the bones are dissolved, so all you taste is a firm healthy fish without the hassle of picking out tiny bones. The marinated fish (with such flavours as sherry, juniper or dill) is eaten locally with the classic beremeal bannock (the dryish bannock, which is the perfect sop to the moist, oily fish), but elsewhere they are served as part of a smørrebrød table or as a starter simply with salad and good bread.

Herring and Potato Gratin

This recipe is loosely based on a much-loved Swedish recipe, Jansson's Temptation, which is, traditionally, a gratin of potatoes, anchovies and cream. I like to use herring fillets and add some wholegrain mustard, which complements the fish perfectly. For speed and ease, ask your fishmonger to skin the herring fillets for you.

Serve the gratin with a crisp green salad.

SERVES 6

1.25kg/2 lb 12 oz large potatoes, peeled
15g/¹⁄₂ oz butter
1 onion, peeled and finely chopped
2 garlic cloves, peeled and chopped
6 large herring fillets, skinned and halved lengthways
600ml/20 fl oz/1 pint pot of single cream
2 tablespoons wholegrain mustard
25g/1 oz fresh breadcrumbs
1 tablespoon extra virgin olive oil
salt and freshly ground black pepper

1 Preheat the oven to 200°C/400°F/Gas 6. Cut the potatoes into very thin slices (I slice mine in my food processor). Melt the butter and gently fry the onion and garlic for 2–3 minutes.

2 Place half the potatoes in a large buttered gratin dish, seasoning well with salt and pepper. Next, tip the onion, garlic and butter all over. Place the herring on top, trying not to overlap. Season again, then top with the remainder of the potatoes. Season again. Mix the cream and mustard together and pour slowly over the dish, ensuring all the potatoes are covered.

3 Cover the dish with buttered foil and cook in the oven for 45 minutes. Remove the foil, sprinkle over the breadcrumbs and drizzle with the oil. Return to the oven for a further 45–50 minutes, or until the potatoes are completely soft. Allow to rest for at least 10 minutes.

Smokie Pots

You can add an egg per pot, if you like: break one into each pot on top of the spinach, season then spoon the sauce over. Bake as instructed below, until the yolk is almost set.

SERVES 4

200g/7 oz spinach, cooked until wilted and patted thoroughly dry
25g/1 oz butter
25g/1 oz plain flour
300ml/10 fl oz/¹/₂ pint milk
1 pair of Arbroath smokies, flesh flaked
40g/1¹/₂ oz freshly grated Parmesan cheese
salt and freshly ground black pepper

1 Preheat the oven to 190°C/375°F/ Gas 5. Place the spinach in the base of each of four ramekins. Season.

2 Melt the butter in a pan, add the flour and stir well. Cook for 1 minute, stirring, then add the milk and cook for 3–4 minutes, or until thickened. Season to taste and add the flaked smokies.

3 Spoon this over the spinach then top with the cheese.

4 Bake for 12–15 minutes, or until golden and bubbling. (If you are adding eggs, cook for no more than 14 minutes.) Eat with plenty of good bread.

Baked Buttered Smokies

The simplest way of eating smokies and the most common in Arbroath.

SERVES 2

2 small pairs of Arbroath smokies
butter

1 Preheat the oven to 180°C/350°F/ Gas 4. Place the smokies on a large sheet of buttered foil and tightly wrap. Bake for 15–20 minutes, or until hot.

2 Unwrap, tuck a knob of butter inside each pair of fish. Rewrap, leave for 2–3 minutes then devour with granary bread and salad.

Hairy Tatties

During visits to Orkney and Shetland, I kept seeing – in butcher's and fishmonger's – packs of salted fish: salt haddock, whiting, tusk and ling. Salt cod and ling were traditionally the most common but cod is scarce nowadays. Tusk is a member of the cod family and has been traditionally very popular in Orkney and Shetland. The salt fish is soaked, boiled and then eaten with mashed potatoes and melted butter (or roasted mutton fat on Shetland).

In Aberdeenshire there is a wonderful dish called Hairy Tatties. The name derives from the technique of constant beating of the tatties to make them dry and almost fibrous ('hairy') in texture. I was taught how to make this dish correctly by Margaret Rutherford who grew up in Fraserburgh but whose parents, the Websters, came from the tiny fishing village of Crovie on the north Banffshire coast, where this dish was commonplace. Margaret also remembers the barrel in the back shed filled with salt herring ('saaty herrin'), which were served with tatties on a regular basis. Margaret's task when Hairy Tatties were being made was to take the drained tatties to the back door and give them a really good shake, until they became almost mealie. (She is unsure why she had to do this outside but recalls her mother insisting the sunshine helped the tattie-shaking procedure!) Hairy Tatties were traditionally served with a sauce made with dried English mustard, but Margaret preferred my idea of using Dijon mustard instead.

If you can only find *bacalao* or the Spanish/Portuguese salt cod for this, that is fine but it is stiffer and more heavily salted, and so soak this for up to 48 hours, changing the water several times.

And you can also make Spanish salt-cod 'fritters' – *bunuelos de bacalao* – with Hairy Tattie leftovers by adding some crushed garlic to the mixture then, with floured hands, shaping into little balls, rolling them in medium oatmeal and deep-frying until golden and crunchy outside. Serve as they do in London's Fino Restaurant with tartare sauce. Yum!

SERVES 4–6

600–700g/1 lb 5 oz–1 lb 9 oz salt fish, such as haddock, ling, tusk or whiting
1.5kg/3 lb 5 oz floury potatoes (unpeeled weight)
75g/2³/4 oz butter
200ml/7 fl oz/¹/3 pint full-fat milk, hot
3 tablespoons Dijon mustard
2 tablespoons chopped parsley
freshly ground black pepper

1 Soak the fish in cold water for anything from 6 to 12 hours before you intend to cook it. During this time, change the water once (more often if you know it is a heavy salt cure).

2 Cover with fresh cold water, bring slowly to the boil then reduce to a simmer, cover and cook slowly for 8–10 minutes then remove. Drain. Once cool enough to handle, flake into chunks, carefully removing the skin and bones.

3 Peel and boil the potatoes until tender then drain well. Mash with the butter and milk, then add mustard and pepper to taste (no salt). Fold in the flaked fish then the parsley. Traditionally milk was drunk with this, but I have to say a nice glass or two of a different 'chilled white' goes down a treat!

Smokie Pâté with Crowdie and Lovage

I love to use crowdie cheese for this, as it has a unique texture that is smooth yet firm and with a sharp, lemony taste. Otherwise you can use ricotta (although it is not as low fat as crowdie, which has only 4.5g per 100g) – the taste is still good but the overall texture will be softer.

If you cannot find lovage, substitute a few celery leaves and the grated zest of half a lemon instead.

SERVES 4–6

1 large Arbroath smokie (or a pair of small smokies), flesh removed
150g/5½ oz crowdie cheese
2 tablespoons lovage leaves
the juice of 1½ lemons
freshly ground black pepper

1 Whiz everything together in a blender (or a food processor, but because it is easy to miss a bone, the blender is more likely to eliminate it than the processor). Taste and add pepper as necessary. (You should not need any salt.)

2 Chill before serving with thick oatcakes or warm bannocks.

Smoked Brandade Tart with Tapenade

You can either use (undyed) smoked haddock or Arbroath smokies for this delicious tart which is inspired by that wonderful Provencal dish *brandade* made of salt cod, potato, garlic and olive oil.

If you cannot find a jar of good commercial tapenade, it is a doddle to make yourself and of course much nicer: simply stone 30 Kalamata or large black olives and whiz with a peeled, halved garlic clove, 3 anchovy fillets, 1 teaspoon Dijon mustard and the juice of half a lemon. Add enough olive oil (about 3 tablespoons) to make a thickish paste. You will not need to add salt.

SERVES 6-8

200g/7 oz plain flour, sifted
25g/1 oz freshly grated Parmesan cheese
125g/4½ oz unsalted butter, diced
1 large free-range egg, beaten
salt and freshly ground black pepper

FOR THE FILLING

500g/1 lb 2 oz undyed smoked haddock fillets (or 1 pair of Arbroath smokies)
150ml/5 fl oz/¼ pint milk
2 garlic cloves, peeled and crushed
2 large free-range eggs
200ml/7 fl oz/⅓ pint crème fraîche
2 tablespoons chopped fresh flat-leaf parsley
the juice and grated zest of 1 unwaxed lemon
extra virgin olive oil
about 3 tablespoons tapenade (black olive paste)

1 For the pastry, place the flour, Parmesan and butter in a food processor with a pinch of salt. Process, then slowly add the egg through the feeder tube. Alternatively, rub in the flour and Parmesan mixture by hand and stir in the egg. Add a couple of drops of water if needed then bring the dough together with your hands and wrap in clingfilm.

2 Chill for an hour or so, then roll out to fit a deep 23cm/9 in tart tin. Prick the base and chill again – preferably overnight.

3 Preheat the oven to 190°C/375°F/ Gas 5. Line the pastry case with foil and fill with baking beans, and bake blind for 15 minutes. Remove foil and beans, and continue to bake for 5–10 minutes more, or until the pastry is just cooked. Remove and cool.

4 To make the filling, place the fish in a pan with the milk and garlic. Bring slowly to the boil. For the smokies, remove the pan from the heat the minute you see bubbles, and cover. For smoked haddock, simmer for about 3 minutes then remove from the heat, and cover. Leave to stand for 10–15 minutes.

5 Remove the fish, reserving the milk. Flake the fish, ensuring there are neither bones nor skin, then place in a food processor with the garlic.

Add the eggs, crème fraîche, parsley, the lemon juice and zest and the warm milk. Process well until you have a soft, creamy consistency.

6 Smear about 3 tablespoons tapenade carefully over the pastry base. Top with the fish mixture then bake for about 40–45 minutes, or until golden brown.

7 Leave for at least 20 minutes then serve warm with a tomato salad.

Smokies Salade Niçoise
Serve with a warm baguette.

SERVES 3–4
crisp salad leaves, washed
3 or 4 large tomatoes, quartered
100g/3½ oz green beans, blanched for 1 minute until *al dente*
3 hard-boiled free-range eggs, peeled and quartered
4–6 waxy salad potatoes, cooked in their skins and quartered
1 pair Arbroath smokies, flesh flaked
a good handful of black olives
50g/1³⁄₄ oz anchovies, drained
5 tablespoons extra virgin olive oil
the juice of 1 lemon
salt and freshly ground black pepper

1 Place the salad leaves in a large salad bowl, then top with the tomatoes, beans, eggs, potatoes and, finally, the smokies. Add the olives and anchovies.

2 Whisk together the oil and lemon juice, season then pour this dressing over the salad just before serving.

Roast Fish with Warm Hummus and Roasted Tomatoes

A Skye fisherman was telling some urban schoolchildren from the mainland about fishing on the island. 'Catching the fish is easy,' he said. 'The hard bit is catching the chips.' Fortunately, most of the children knew it was safe to laugh.

SERVES 4

4 thick fillets of haddock or other white fish, such as gurnard, rock turbot
   or cod loin
extra virgin olive oil
about 150g/5¹/₂ oz cherry tomatoes on the vine
400g/14 oz chickpeas, drained
2 garlic cloves, peeled and chopped
the juice of 2 lemons
2 tablespoons tahini
2 teaspoons ground cumin
1 heaped tablespoon coriander leaves
salt and freshly ground black pepper

1 Preheat the oven to 220°C/425°F/Gas 7. Place the fish on an oiled baking tray (tucking any thin end under to make a thicker parcel if using a haddock fillet). Top with the tomatoes then drizzle generously with oil. Season with salt and pepper.

2 Roast at the top of the oven for about 15 minutes, or until the fish is just cooked. (Test with the tip of a sharp knife: the flesh should no longer be translucent in the thickest part.)

3 For the hummus, place the chickpeas, garlic, lemon juice, tahini, cumin and coriander leaves in a food processor. Blend until smooth. Add enough oil to make a thickish purée – about 4 tablespoons. 'Loosen' the mixture if it is too thick with a couple of tablespoons of warm water. Season to taste and tip into a shallow ovenproof dish. Cover with foil and place in the oven beneath the fish for about 15 minutes, or until just warm.

4 To serve, place a dollop of hummus on to a warm plate, top with the fish then the tomatoes, drizzling over the pan juices. Serve with warm pitta bread.

Potted Herring

This is my mother's recipe for potted (or soused) herring, which is a very typical dish eaten at teatime with salad and potatoes or brown bread and butter.

My fishmonger advises using smaller herring – as these are the sweetest and so no sugar is required in the sousing. The vinegar and water solution will also dissolve the tiny feather bones easily in smaller fish. Larger ones have harder bones, which take longer to dissolve.

See also the similar recipe for 'Pickled Herring in Seaweed' on page 144.

SERVES 4–6

6–8 boned (small) herring, about 75g/2³⁄4 oz each, prepared weight, cleaned
1 medium onion, peeled and sliced
150ml /5 fl oz/¹⁄4 pint white wine vinegar
10–12 black peppercorns
1 blade of mace
2 fresh bay leaves
salt and freshly ground black pepper

1 Preheat the oven to 180°C/350°F/ Gas 4. Season the herring inside with salt and pepper.

2 Place half the onion in the base of an ovenproof dish. Roll up the herring (with the skin side out and starting from the tail end) and place on top, packing tightly together, to keep them rolled up. Top with the remaining onion slices.

3 Place the vinegar, an equal quantity of water, peppercorns, mace and bay leaves in a saucepan. Bring to the boil then pour over the herring; the liquid should almost cover the fish. (Don't worry that the fins are still on – they will come away easily once cooked. Trying to remove them before cooking will result only in a large hole in the back.)

4 Cover tightly and bake for 25 minutes then remove and leave to cool, still covered, until cold.

Herring in Oatmeal

This is a traditional dish I remember from my childhood, either served at teatime or breakfast. My mother remembers going to the meal-shop in Dundee before her mother – my Granny Ward – fried herring for tea.

Herring is best between June and September in Scotland, and so oatmeal herring is best served with freshly dug potatoes, earth still clinging to their skins, for a true taste of summer. You can use either pinhead or medium oatmeal; pinhead gives a crunchier texture, but medium coats more evenly.

SERVES 2–4

50–60g/1³/₄–2¹/₄ oz medium or pinhead oatmeal
4 boned herrings, about 90g/3¹/₄ oz each, prepared weight, cleaned
25–40g/1–1¹/₂ oz butter
salt and freshly ground black pepper

1 Place the oatmeal on a plate and season with salt and pepper. Press the fish into it. Coat both sides. (If it has been freshly filleted for you the oatmeal should stick well, but if it has been done earlier in the day, swish it briefly under a cold tap, shake dry then coat in the oatmeal.)

2 To fry, heat the butter in a frying pan until hot then add the fish, flesh-side down. After about 3 minutes turn over and continue cooking for about 3 minutes, or until cooked through. Serve on warm plates with new potatoes and either mustard or salsa verde.

Great-Auntie Effie, Granny Anderson and Great-Auntie Maggie, West Ferry beach near Dundee, 1917

As farmer David Ismail stands on a hill overlooking his 1,500 acre farm, which dates back to the seventeenth century, he points at the fields and says, 'They are designed to convert poor grass on the hills into meat – the best meat in the world; and the girls also convert it into milk.' This is nature at its most fundamental, as 'they' are his herd of pedigree Aberdeen Angus cattle, those noble-looking creatures that used to be known simply as 'Angus Blacks'.

The story of probably the world's most sought-after beef breed is interesting. There is mention of black cattle in Scotland in our earliest manuscripts and carvings on old stones. But it took an Angus farmer in 1808, Hugh Watson from Newtyle just north of Dundee, to select the right animals to create the breed of black, hornless, compactly built beef cattle that we have today, even though nowadays they tend to be larger than two centuries ago. The name 'Aberdeen' was introduced, instead of simply 'Angus Black', because a couple of Aberdeenshire farmers after Hugh Watson then continued to develop the breed; but to me, a Dundonian, I like to think that the world's best beef originated very near to my home town.

David Ismail's organic herd of 250 (200 pedigree, 50 cross bred) roam all over the grassland and heather hills of his farm near Glenfarg in Perthshire; sometimes bulls and cows together with calves, rather like life on a commune, sometimes young bulls all together in a field. My natural aversion to (or is that terror of?) bulls was tested when David insisted I enter a field of young bulls as he patted them fondly and described the classic shape of the Aberdeen Angus: well-sprung ribs and broad, deep-layered backs under a coat of sleek black. And he explained that their fat is evenly spread over the frame and marbled through the muscle. Both their smooth, soft (not sinewy) muscle and their natural ability to marble make Aberdeen Angus not only unique but also sublime. But before anyone thinks this natural marbling means fatty meat, compare the average 20 per cent Aberdeen Angus's fat with a Japanese Waygu's potential 70 per cent maximum!

And when one considers the diet of these beasts, it is easy to see why they are so splendid, not only to behold but to eat. The calves have only mother's milk until mid-October (having been born some 6–7 months earlier), then they all eat the same: sugar beet pellets, silage and dark grains. This last is draff (ground up malted barley left over after mashing) mixed with evaporated pot ale. The dark grains are dry, as they are pelletised. These by-products of the whisky industry also lend Aberdeen Angus its particular Scottish character. This is meat with a unique heritage and most attuned to its environment: they calve easily (on the hills), are early to mature and are also hardy enough to stay outside all winter as they feed on the grass, kale (David's farm has large kale fields), silage and those dark grains, which, I am assured by whisky expert Dave Broom, have virtually no alcohol left in them. But perhaps the word 'virtually' might explain the impossibly contented demeanour of these magnificent beasts.

The next stage in the chain of prime-quality Scottish beef is, of course, the butcher. I went to visit one of Scotland's finest, David Craig of Robertson's in Dundee (he has a shop in the city centre and one in the seaside suburb of Broughty Ferry).

He told me that in July 2004, Scotch Beef was awarded Protected Geographical Indication (PGI) status by the EC which means cattle have to be born, reared throughout their lives, slaughtered and dressed in Scotland. For David, as with other butchers of integrity, it is not just the expensive cuts of meat that are top quality, but the cheaper cuts too. So whether you offer a grand five-rib roast for a special occasion or just some mince for tea, it is always delicious. David's mince, for example, was found in a Food Standards Agency random survey to be one of the top three in the UK for fat content (his had 3.5 per cent fat; some supermarkets had over 25 per cent). He says the secret is to seam the beef out (remove the interconnective tissue, which many butchers and supermarket meat departments leave in). He uses only top of shin and neck of shoulder for his mince. For his steak pies he uses thick flank, diced shoulder and topside, and for his award-winning individual Scotch pies, minced shoulder. This follows the trend nowadays for all Scotch pies to be made with beef not mutton as was the case in my parents' childhoods.

But it was a peculiarly Scottish institution I wanted to check out: the lorne sausage. An uncased beef sausage, its distinctive characteristic is its square shape; indeed it is often referred to as 'square sausage'. There is no water added to the mixture, making it a dense but supremely tasty sausage when well made. Ah, there's the rub; so many Scots equate lorne sausage with poor quality because many butchers over the years have made it with scraps as a form of economy. (Some supermarket offerings have a depressing 60 per cent beef; one dreads to think what constitutes the remaining 40 per cent.)

I watched David Craig make his, mincing shoulder, neck and shin of beef once, adding a special seasoning and a small bowlful of rusk then mincing again before pressing into an oblong lorne sausage pan. This is then turned out raw and left to set for a couple of hours before being sliced. The result, an exceedingly beefy sausage (minimum 85 per cent beef), is a joy. It is a sausage to be proud of, and, carefully cooked, one that deserves to be up there with the best traditionally cured bacon and free-range eggs for breakfast. (Overcook it, however, and it becomes rubbery, as it is so lean.) Indeed the classic way to serve it – and this is David Craig's favourite – is in a soft morning roll (not well fired or crisp) with a fried egg on top. This takes me back to my childhood and makes me appreciate that simple food, done well, needs little embellishment; it also needs to be shouted about. Bring back lorne sausage to its rightful place at the Scottish breakfast table!

And as for lunch, unless it is a magnificent rib roast on Sunday, I recommend Dundee's famous Saturday lunch: a Scotch Pie and Buster Peas (marrowfat peas cooked until soft). The quality of the pie is of course crucial and, fortunately, to balance all those grim offerings on sale in national chain-store bakeries and some supermarkets, good bakers and butchers produce pies to be proud of.

Baker and butcher Alan Stuart of Buckhaven on the central Fife coast uses minced beef flank in his award-winning Scotch pies. And the phrase 'award-winning' is apposite: Alan founded the World Scotch Pie Championships in 1999. I was fortunate enough to help judge the 'Savouries' a couple of years ago: yes, all 123 of them. Once our judgely huddle had ploughed their way (at first with keen and eager palates) through such delicacies as Sheep and Neep Pie with its wonderful peppery topping, Stovie Pie with its delicious onion-laden filling, and Lasagne Pie (just what you might imagine but better), our palates were more than a little jaded. But just the sight of the Cow Pie (authentic Desperate Dan-style with integral pastry horns), was enough to ensure our sense of humour remained intact.

The good thing about this competition is that as the number of entries has risen, so has the standard. The chances of finding a perfectly crafted pastry case (crisp not hard) containing a substantial meaty filling (totally devoid of gristle or grease, with just enough gravy to moisten) are higher than ever. Nowadays craft bakers and butchers take this competition so seriously some spend most of the year fine-tuning their pie recipes. And this I find so encouraging, not only for the sake of our culinary heritage (we Scots have eaten Scotch pies for centuries) but also to dispel that old chestnut about the poor Scots diet. It is only poor because of the ubiquity of refined, processed foods, laden with additives and preservatives.

The Pie Awards lunch had an almost surreal start: as the shrill drone of the bagpipes settled into a pleasing skirl, the piper entered and a reverent hush fell over the expectant crowd. And as the silver asthet was held aloft, behind him a piper strode proudly around the room. With great ceremony, a dram was given to the piper and the asthet bearer, then the poem 'Tae a Scotch Pie' was recited. And on that lofty platter was not a pre-Burns Supper haggis, but a hillock of golden-crusted Scotch pies. This was, after all, the World Scotch Pie Championships Awards and, rather like the Oscars, there was tension in the air. There were 65 entries in the Scotch pie section, 56 in bridies and that astonishing 123 in savouries. And everyone present hoped their pie had won the Gold.

The sight of this glorious pile of pies encouraged Alan Stuart to tell me about the possibly apocryphal tale heard on a Saturday in one of his Buckhaven baker shops. (Bear in mind that, locally, Scotch pies are treated, sacred-cow-like, with hushed reverence.) One of the Saturday girls had made a fabulous window display of Scotch pies, not unlike a *croquembouche* in a pyramid shape, which attracted silent, murmured praise. When one customer (obviously not local) verbally congratulated her on her 'window display', the girl retorted, 'But it's not a window display; it's a Buckhaven wedding cake.'

Anderson, Hadden and Henderson family picnic in the Borders, 1958

Brönies and Bannocks

This is Shetland's answer to the hamburger in a bun – but much tastier. The brönie (not to be confused with Shetland's Brunnies – wholemeal, plain flour or oat girdle bread) is a kind of meat patty. It is made from sassermaet (also known as 'saucermeat'), minced beef and onions. Sassermaet is Shetland's sausagemeat – with a difference. Made primarily by butchers, it is still occasionally made at home. It is basically raw salted beef that is mixed with fat and spiced with pepper, allspice, cinnamon, cloves and sometimes ginger or nutmeg. It is formed into a round mound or square sausage, not unlike lorne sausage, although the latter is less heavily spiced. It is fried (without fat, as it is has sufficient in its mix) and served with fried onion, egg or boiled potatoes.

Anne Eunson, from Unst, the most northerly Shetland island, told me about the bannocks she was brought up on, from the regular bere and floury (pronounced 'floorie') bannocks to a 'huffsie': a big flour bannock cooked in a roasting tin. This recipe calls for the smaller floury bannocks which are similar to soda scones.

SERVES 3–4

150g/5¹/₂ oz sassermaet (or sausagemeat, preferably beef)
150g/5¹/₂ oz lean minced steak
¹/₄ medium onion, peeled and finely chopped
25g/1 oz medium oatmeal
3 or 4 floury bannocks (or *Soda Scones*, see page 62)
salt and freshly ground black pepper

1 Combine the sassermaet or sausagemeat, minced steak, onion and oatmeal, then add only a tiny amount of salt and pepper, as sassermaet is well seasoned. Using your hands, mould into three or four small cakes, flatten out with your hands then chill for an hour or so.

2 Fry the brönies gently until cooked through (I do not use any fat as there is enough in the sassermaet, but if you do not have a reliable pan, you might need a splash of oil). This will take 10–15 minutes depending on the thickness. Ensure that they are cooked through.

3 Meanwhile, warm the bannocks and place a brönie in each. (I also like a smear of black olive tapenade on one side of the bannock.) Serve with a tomato salad.

Roast Rib of Beef With Skirlie and Claret Gravy

Roast rib of beef is one of those most glorious centrepieces to any table. Usually served down south with Yorkshire pudding, I prefer skirlie and a good gutsy claret gravy, the latter a nod towards the claret-drinking past of the Scots, established during the thirteenth century. For it was in 1295 that the Auld Alliance was signed, giving the Scottish merchants the privilege of selecting the first choice of Bordeaux's finest wines (a privilege that was not extended to their fellow Britons down south, much to their chagrin).

The skirlie is a great favourite – a rather more crunchy white pudding made of similar ingredients, which are simply onions and oatmeal. White puddings take me back to my university days in Dundee when, late at night, after perhaps more than one small drink in the Student Union, we would head straight for either Sweaty Betty's or Greasy Pete's on the Hawkhill for a fish supper or – my favourite – a white pudding supper. Just the job to soak up the evening's libations.

SERVES 8–10

4–5 bone rib of beef
2 heaped tablespoons plain flour
200ml/7 fl oz/¹/₃ pint claret
600ml/20 fl oz/1 pint beef stock, hot
salt and freshly ground black pepper

FOR THE SKIRLIE

75g/2³/₄ oz dripping (or 40g/1¹/₂ oz butter plus 2 tablespoons olive oil)
2 medium onions, peeled and finely chopped
175g/6 oz coarse oatmeal (or half pinhead, half medium)

1 Preheat the oven to 230°C/450°F/Gas 8. Ensure the beef is at room temperature by removing it from the fridge at least an hour before cooking. Place in a roasting tin, season all over then place in the oven, without any extra fat, for 15 minutes. Reduce the heat to 170°C/325°F/Gas 3 and continue to roast for 17 minutes per 500g/1 lb 2 oz (this will give you medium-rare). Once it is cooked to your liking, remove the beef carefully to a carving board while you make the gravy. Rest the beef, loosely covered in foil, for at least 20 minutes.

2 To make the gravy, spoon off the excess fat from the tin, to leave only the dark juices, about 2–3 tablespoons. Place over a direct heat and add the flour. Stir well, scraping up all the bits, then slowly add the claret and then the stock. Change from a wooden spoon to a balloon whisk and whisk for about 8–10 minutes, or until you have a smooth gravy. Taste for seasoning and continue cooking gently, whisking all the time, until piping hot and smooth.

3 To make the skirlie, melt the fat in a frying pan then gently fry the onions for 10 minutes, or until softened. Add the oatmeal, and cook over a medium heat, stirring, until toasted and crumbly, about 10 minutes. Season to taste then serve piping hot.

4 Carve the beef and serve with the claret gravy, some skirlie, roast potatoes and green vegetables.

Inky-Pinky

The original Inky-Pinky appeared in Mistress Meg Dods' recipe book (from her 1829 *Manual*) then republished in F. Marian McNeill's *The Scots Kitchen* in 1929. This old recipe, using leftover roast beef, had boiled carrots and a shake of vinegar in it, and it was all simmered on the stove until hot. My recipe omits the carrots (I loathe reheated boiled carrots) and has a little mustard for added zing. It is also done in the oven so you can set about preparing the mash. The nineteenth-century Inky-Pinky was served with 'sippets' (small pieces of toasted or fried bread).

SERVES 3–4
400–500g/14oz–1 lb 2 oz sliced cold roast beef (or lamb)
1 large onion, peeled and thinly sliced
2 teaspoons Dijon mustard
300–400ml/10–14 fl oz gravy

1 Preheat the oven to 180°C/350°F/Gas 4. Place the meat in a wide, shallow oven dish and sprinkle over the onion slices. Mix the mustard into the gravy and spoon over.

2 Cover with foil and bake in the oven for about 40 minutes, or until piping hot. Serve with mash and green veg.

Fife Miners' Stew with Soda Scones

Alan Stuart, the baker in Buckhaven, told me of this wonderful dish, stew with soda scones. For about a century, until the 1970s, when mining was of crucial importance in south Fife, this dish was a tradition in most miners' homes on Sunday for late breakfast after church, their one and only day off. The stew was cooked very slowly on the stove overnight and the scones made fresh just before the meal.

My stew recipe is a little more elaborate, perhaps, but utterly delicious served with the scones below, or just with mash or baked potatoes.

The scones are also wonderful served warm with butter and jam for tea.

FEEDS 4 HUNGRY MINERS
1 tablespoon extra virgin olive oil
1 large onion, peeled and chopped
2 fat garlic cloves, peeled and chopped
2 heaped tablespoons plain flour, seasoned
1kg/2 lb 4 oz stewing steak, diced
2 heaped tablespoons tomato purée
4 large thick carrots, peeled and cut into huge chunks
4 large thick parsnips, peeled and cut into huge chunks
200ml/7 fl oz/¹/₃ pint red wine
300ml/10 fl oz/¹/₂ pint beef stock
the zest of 1 small orange
salt and freshly ground black pepper

1 Preheat the oven to 150°C/300°F/ Gas 2. Heat the oil in a large flameproof casserole then gently fry the onion and garlic for a couple of minutes, or until softened.

2 Place the flour in a large plastic bag, add the meat and toss around to coat. Tip into the casserole with all remaining ingredients. Stir, bring to the boil then cover. Place in the oven for 4 hours, stirring once. Season to taste, then serve with soda scones.

Soda Scones

When cooked in the round and not cut into quarters as these are, this is like Orkney's floury (pronounced 'floorie') bannock.

MAKES 4

250g/9 oz self-raising flour
1/2 teaspoon bicarbonate of soda
1/2 teaspoon salt
2 teaspoons golden caster sugar
1 medium free-range egg
30ml/1 fl oz sunflower oil, plus extra for greasing
about 175ml/6 fl oz milk (or about 200ml/7 fl oz/1/3 pint buttermilk)

1 First heat your girdle (griddle; or heavy frying pan) to medium hot, smearing with a little oil.

2 Sift the flour and soda into a bowl with the salt and sugar. Make a well in the centre and add the egg, oil and enough milk (or buttermilk) to combine to a soft dough. Do not overwork.

3 Tip on to a floured board and shape (without kneading) into a round about 22cm/8½ in diameter (it should be about 2cm/¾ in thick). Using a floured knife, cut into quarters. Dust lightly with flour and transfer carefully to the hot girdle. Cook for about 5 minutes (by which time they will have risen and will have formed a fabulous brown crust underneath) then carefully flip each over. Continue to cook until done (when you press down lightly there should be no liquid oozing out the sides, and the edges will be dry). Transfer to a wire rack and serve warm with the stew.

Steaks with Broad Bean and Mint Salsa Verde

During a visit to one of the most stunning places on earth, the island of Tiree in the Inner Hebrides (with the whitest sand and the bluest of crystal-clear water), I went to see Nan-the-Butcher in the village of Scarinish. Only local beef and lamb are sold – both cattle and sheep raised, finished and slaughtered on the island. Beside the butcher's shop is the tiny abattoir where they slaughter the animals about once a week. Then the beef is hung for three weeks, giving the most wonderful flavour. In the Scarinish Hotel, I ate Nan's beef as fillet steak with a side serving of haggis; and also very simply as seared sirloin steak, tasty and perfectly cooked, with no sauce, just salad. With meat this good, rich or creamy sauces are unnecessary; this simple salsa is just right.

SERVES 2

2 rib-eye steaks
150g/5½ oz frozen broad beans (or about 450g/1 lb fresh pods) or peas
15g/½ oz fresh mint
1 heaped tablespoon capers
½ tablespoon red wine vinegar
about 2 teaspoons horseradish sauce
about 4 tablespoons extra virgin olive oil, plus extra for rubbing
salt and freshly ground black pepper

1 Ensure the steaks are at room temperature. To make the salsa, if using fresh beans or peas, remove them from the pods. Cook fresh or frozen until just tender but still vivid green then drain and run under the cold tap to arrest the colour. Pat thoroughly dry.

2 Put into a food processor with the mint, capers, vinegar and 2 teaspoons horseradish, and process until combined. Add enough oil to form a coarse paste. Season to taste and add extra horseradish, if you like.

3 Rub olive oil into the steaks and set aside for 10–15 minutes while you heat a griddle pan to hot.

4 Slap on the steaks, season and reduce the heat to medium-high. Do not touch the meat for 4 minutes, then turn over and continue to cook for 3–4 minutes (for medium-rare) depending on the thickness. Allow the meat to rest on a warm plate for 3–4 minutes before serving with a dollop of the salsa and a baked potato.

Scotch Pie and Buster Peas

Most Dundonians' Saturday lunch – certainly when my parents were growing up and very often now before going to the football – was a Scotch pie (sometimes a Forfar bridie) with buster peas. And although traditionally buster peas were simply dried marrowfat peas soaked then boiled until tender and seasoned with salt, pepper and vinegar, I cook dried split peas (for quicker cooking) in stock and add an onion for extra flavour. Do not mash down too much at the end, as you want the split peas mainly as they are. Remember this is not mushy peas; this is buster peas, which were also served famously with chips, called 'lang tatties' by many Dundonians.

SERVES 4–6
300g/10½ oz dried split peas, soaked overnight
1 onion, peeled and chopped
700ml/1¼ pints hot beef stock
4–6 best (butcher's) Scotch pies
sherry vinegar (optional)
salt and freshly ground black pepper

1 Place the drained split peas in a pan with the onion and hot stock. Bring to the boil (do not add any salt) and boil vigorously for 5 minutes, skimming off any scum on the surface. Reduce the heat to low and simmer, covered, for about 40 minutes, or until tender.

2 Meanwhile, preheat the oven to 180°C/350°F/Gas 4. Add salt and pepper to taste to the peas and mash them down a little, but ensure you have plenty of whole peas left.

3 Heat the pies in the oven for 10–15 minutes, or until hot, and serve with the Buster Peas. Add a shake of vinegar to the peas just before serving, if you like.

Lorne Sausage Casserole

The traditional time for lorne sausage is breakfast: simply dry-fry in a hot pan until just done then plonk into a morning roll – with or without a (runny-yolked) fried egg on top. My cousin Dave's wife Elisabeth has an extra treat: in between the sausage and egg, she puts a tattie (potato) scone. The scone absorbs any runny yolk that might otherwise dribble down your chin.

Bacon-curer Andrew Ramsay in Carluke makes a delicious pork lorne sausage, again with only prime meat and little else. Although not the traditional beef, it is a welcome addition to the lorne sausage family.

This casserole recipe is a modern adaptation of a student dish. In the next door flat to mine at Dundee university the 'house special' – devised by flat-member Gordon Bennett – was raw lorne sausage in a casserole topped by carrots and sweetcorn and the lot swathed in a tin of condensed tomato soup, then baked until bubbling. That was living! My recipe uses a fresh tomato sauce and I like to brown the sausage first, but the basic components are still there. I can personally do without the sweetcorn, but in keeping with the spirit of 1970s student fare, I give it as an optional extra.

For the fresh tomato sauce, gently fry a couple of garlic cloves and half an onion in olive oil for 2–3 minutes then tip in a 400g/14 oz tin of tomatoes, season and simmer for 10 minutes before puréeing.

SERVES 3–4

3 or 4 slices quality lorne sausage, cut in half
250g/9 oz spinach, wilted in a little water until just soft and drained well
1/2 x 300g/10 1/2 oz tin of sweetcorn, drained (optional)
350g/12 oz fresh tomato sauce
75g/2 3/4 oz mozzarella, sliced
sea salt and freshly ground black pepper

1 Preheat the oven to 190°C/375°F/ Gas 5. Heat a frying pan until hot then add the lorne sausage and brown on both sides (1 minute or so on each side).

2 Meanwhile, place the spinach in the base of an oven dish, season with salt and pepper then place the sausage on top. Scatter the sweetcorn, if using, over the top. Spoon the tomato sauce over, then top with the sliced mozzarella. Season and drizzle over a little oil.

3 Bake in the oven for about 30 minutes, or until bubbling.

4 Serve with mash or a baked potato.

Ginger and Soy-marinated Fillet of Beef

I use a tail-end piece of fillet for this tasty but very easy dish.
If you do not use the tail end, you might need to add a couple
of minutes on to the cooking time, as it will be thicker.

Serve barely warm with Chinese noodles, or cold with salad.

SERVES 4

1 tablespoon extra virgin olive oil
400–500g/14 oz–1 lb 2 oz tail-end fillet of beef
2 tablespoons soy sauce
1 heaped tablespoon freshly grated root ginger
1 tablespoon roasted sesame oil
2 tablespoons white wine or rice vinegar
salt and freshly ground black pepper

1 Preheat the oven to 200°C/400°F/ Gas 6. Heat the olive oil in a frying pan (preferably one that will go into the oven) and, once hot, add the beef. Season and then brown all over, for 4–5 minutes. Transfer to a roasting tin if necessary and place in the oven for 15 minutes for each 500g/1 lb 2 oz.

2 Meanwhile, combine the remaining ingredients in a bowl that will be large enough to fit the beef in snugly. Place the beef and pan juices into the bowl, and make sure the marinade covers the meat. Cover with clingfilm and leave for 10 minutes. Then remove the clingfilm and leave to marinate for a further 20 minutes or so, spooning over the marinade often. Serve sliced with some marinade.

Del the sheepdog bounds to the top of the hill on his master's command to round up the sheep. After several frantic zigzags around them, they end up in a line like dancing girls at the Folies-Bergères, except that in place of feathers there is wool. Lots of it. These Shetland sheep resemble the sheep young children draw: thin, spindly legs with a barrel-load of wool on top. And as the line approaches, Ronnie Eunson continues to give Del his commands: 'Away back!' until the dog finally crouches down behind his charges.

The pure-bred native Shetland sheep (some 500 of them), reared on Ronnie's organic farm, graze on the fields that run from the hilltops right down to the sea. This ancient breed (Neolithic sheep bones reveal its ancestry here) grazes on heather grassland that might contain wild flowers and herbs such as wild thyme, violets, orchids, primroses or bird's foot trefoil. Seaweed is a part of many of the Shetland sheep's diet. Ronnie explained to me how they somehow – innately – know when the tide is ebbing, and that is when they come down to the shore to graze. And so the seaweed not only provides the animals with essential minerals (they only start going down to the shore at the end of the year when there is less grass) it also gives an additional flavour to the meat, which has been proved to have unique health-giving properties.

And once Del has released the flock from his hypnotic gaze, the sheep bound back up the hill (I like to think, to enjoy the striking view over Clift Sound, south of Shetland's ancient capital, Scalloway, towards the island of Foula 25 miles west) and I quiz Ronnie about these unique health benefits. Studies some years ago found that the meat from the native Shetland breeds has high levels of CLA (conjugated linoleic acid), which has been shown to reduce the risk of cardiovascular disease and have an inhibiting effect on cancer growth. The lambs that are traditionally raised, fed on these heather pastures, also show higher levels of omega-3 fatty acids than other sheep. The Shetland breed also has a healthier balance of omega-3 to omega-6 fatty acids than other breeds. All in all, once butchered, a mouthful of good health!

As I sat in the Eunsons' farmhouse discussing native sheep, Ronnie told me about the cold mutton (roasted until still pink and moist) and bere bannocks he took to a recent UK Slow Food AGM and how much everyone loved them. In Ronnie's words, people are voting with their taste buds. His meat is so good, it needs little in terms of add-ons when cooking, but the older it gets the more flavourings can be used to complement the strong flavour of what becomes mutton. Ronnie's wife Anne also told me that, although as a child she was brought up on Shetland's salt mutton (saat mutton) and salt fish (saat fish: whether piltocks – a member of the saithe family – or herring or haddock), her taste for these traditional salt products has waned. And reestit (cured) mutton is always made from mutton not lamb. Ronnie has tried it with lamb and 'it doesna work', so why bother? Shetland lamb also now has the PDO (Protected Designation of Origin) status that Ronnie reckons is welcome because the native products have something very special to offer the market place. It is a richly flavoured meat, and, as Edinburgh butcher Sandy Crombie comments, 'rather like tasting good malt whiskies from different areas, it absorbs everything from the area and embodies it'. This native lamb with its long pedigree is not only healthy, its unique flavour is unsurpassed: a taste of both land and sea.

Blackface ewes with Scottish mule and Blackface lambs at the Dick's Borders Farm, overlooking the Moorfoot Hills

Nearer to home, I went to visit the Dick's farm in the Borders. Linda Dick is known among food connoisseurs in Scotland for her chickens, but her husband's lamb is also superb. Jim took me on a tour of their 1,200-acre hill farm to see some of their 1,000 ewes and 1,600 lambs. Half of the flock is Scottish Blackface ('blackies'), which, as the only sheep here with horns, at least make them instantly recognisable to me, the city slicker. The blackies always have spirit and, according to Jim, who is as much philosopher as hill farmer (although he seems pretty good at that too), 'spirit equals durability', which is essential for the high grazing: the Dick farmland is as high as 1,500 ft. On the opposite side of the metaphorical fence to the spirited blackies, Jim places the Texal cross ewes. These he reckons might be hardy physically but not in spirit. And so the cross-breeding of sheep is not only for their size and the ease of adapting to certain land or weather conditions but also for their character. All fascinating stuff, particularly when Jim moved on to terminology: a lamb is a lamb from birth to 1 January, then it is a hogg (2 January to mid June), then a gimmer which is a clipped hogg (are you following?) and finally a ewe once she has had her lambs.

A quick tour of the cross-bred sheep made me even more confused at first but when you realise that, ideal though the blackies are for this terrain, the dressed weight of their carcass is never more than 18kg and usually only 16kg, they make little financial sense. Which is why they are crossed with a Blue-faced Leicester ram and the Scottish Mule is born. These can have carcasses of up to 22kg. As we speed across the hills of the farm, in the middle of an unusual heatwave, Jim tells me that, sadly, a couple of his lambs have already died of heatstroke. And one winter 5 years ago he lost 30 Blackies to a snow storm. Although they know innately how to find shelter from snowdrifts, suddenly at night the wind changed direction and they were buried under the snow. That is the vagaries of British weather of course; but it is also the plight of the hill farmer. Jim and Linda, helped by their sons Ian and Colin, tackle it each day with dedication – and humour. And you need plenty of that as a hill sheep farmer nowadays.

Tattie Soup with Reestit Mutton

Reestit mutton is cured mutton: salted for some 10 days then hung up on hooks to dry, traditionally over the peat fire. An old recipe I found on Shetland calls for two sheep to be salted (it omits the butchering thereof!) then left in a barrel of water with saltpetre, ginger, cinnamon and pepper for two weeks before being removed and hung to dry. Another recipe calls for it to be brined in a bucket with one potato in the water – salt is added until the potato floats to the top; that's when you know you've put in enough. It is then left for three weeks. In the Globe Butcher's in Lerwick, their reestit mutton is cured only in salt (no spices), for three weeks, before being hung and dried.

After some time, the mutton looks rather like salt cod, with an ivory hue and a stiff cardboard feel. Some people have it hanging there for so long they wrap it in newspapers to prevent the dust settling. It is then sliced very thinly, soaked, then fried with onions. Or – best of all – made into this most delicious soup. The simplicity of the ingredients belies the fabulous flavour. Reestit mutton really is worth seeking out, as the flavour it gives to this soup is incomparable. Remember to add no salt; it will still end up perfectly seasoned. Traditionally eaten with the reestit mutton sliced and served on the side, the slices are also occasionally added to the soup just before serving.

Reestit mutton was traditionally eaten during the winter months when there was little fresh meat, and is most readily available in butchers' shops around Christmas. On my last trip to Shetland I was given some reestit mutton with the date on their curing, by Lorna Grains, from Vidlin in the north of the mainland. The Globe Butcher's sell it from September through to April. But it also freezes well.

SERVES 6

400g–500g/14 oz–1 lb 2 oz piece of reestit mutton
1 onion, peeled
2–3 large carrots, peeled
600g/1 lb 5 oz potatoes (unpeeled weight)
400g/14 oz turnip (swede) (unpeeled weight)
freshly ground black pepper

1 Place the mutton in a large pan and cover with cold water (about 1.7 litres/3 pints). Bring to the boil and simmer, covered, for about 30 minutes while chopping all the vegetables into good-size chunks. Add them to the pan.

2 Return to the boil and cook, covered, until everything is tender, about 20–25 minutes. Remove the meat and cut off slices. Put on to a warmed serving plate. Purée or whiz the soup until smooth, then season to taste with freshly ground black pepper (*no* salt). Serve piping hot, with the plate of sliced meat on the side.

Lamb Paste

The idea for this recipe came from Christine Hall, mother of Linda Dick, chicken farmer and wife of Jim Dick, the Borders lamb farmer. (Ignore any connotations of the word 'paste' from the Famous Five and the 1950s – and think pâté.)

It is ideal to do on a Monday after a delicious Sunday roast of lamb. Serve with warm bread or toast and salad.

SERVES 6
about 350g/12 oz leftover roast lamb, trimmed
1 tablespoon mint jelly
150g/5½ oz light cream cheese
salt and freshly ground black pepper

1 Whiz everything together in a food processor and add seasoning.

2 Chill to firm up a little before serving.

Roast Lamb with Warm Butter Bean and Mint Purée and Black Pudding

This combination of flavours might not be classic or traditional but it is one I adore. Butter beans were a great childhood favourite of mine, since they were a Dundee staple. When my parents were growing up they were often served with beef or mutton stews or with steak pie. I enhance the beans with some cumin and mint, for a hint of Middle Eastern flavouring, but the slice of butcher's best black pudding on top brings the entire dish back to being British comfort food at its best.

SERVES 6–8

1 large leg of lamb, about 2.5kg–3kg/5 lb 8 oz–6 lb 8 oz
3 garlic cloves, peeled
2 x 400g/14 oz butter beans, drained
4 tablespoons extra virgin olive oil, plus extra for drizzling
3 tablespoons fresh mint
2 teaspoons ground cumin
the juice of 1 lemon
400g/14 oz black pudding, sliced
sea salt and freshly ground black pepper

1 Preheat the oven to 220°C/425°F/ Gas 7. Set the lamb in a roasting tin. Cut 2 garlic cloves into slivers and insert into the lamb, all over. Season with salt and pepper.

2 Roast in the oven for 20 minutes, then reduce the heat to 190°C/375°F/ Gas 5 and continue to cook for 20 minutes per 500g/1 lb 2 oz, basting a couple of times. Transfer to a carving board, cover with foil and rest for 15–20 minutes while you make gravy in the roasting tin.

3 For the bean purée, place the beans, oil, the remaining garlic, mint, cumin and lemon juice in a food processor.

Blend, adding enough warm water (4–5 tablespoons) until a purée forms. Season to taste and tip into a flat bowl. Drizzle some olive oil all over and reheat gently just before serving. (I microwave until warm, not piping hot.)

4 Smear a little oil into a frying pan and fry the black pudding for a couple of minutes on each side. Keep warm.

5 Carve the lamb and serve on top of a spoonful of bean purée. Top with a slice of black pudding, with gravy in a jug on the table.

Braised Shoulder of Lamb with Anchovies and Rosemary

This is a wonderful slow-braised lamb recipe that comes with its own gravy. And do not be put off by the anchovies: they simply add a gloriously savoury tang to the dish. Serve with roast potatoes and a green vegetable.

SERVES 6

1 tablespoon extra virgin olive oil
whole shoulder of lamb on the bone, about 1.8kg/4 lb
2 fat garlic cloves, peeled and chopped
3–4 stalks of rosemary, leaves removed and chopped
100ml/3¹/₂ fl oz red wine vinegar
8 large or 10 medium anchovy fillets, finely snipped
salt and freshly ground black pepper

1 Preheat the oven to 180°C/350°F/ Gas 4. Heat the oil in a large casserole dish then brown the meat all over. Remove the meat and add the garlic and rosemary. Stir well then add the vinegar. Bubble on a high heat for a minute or so then add 150ml/5 fl oz/ ¹/₄ pint cold water and bring to the boil. Season then return the meat to the pan. Baste then cover: either with a lid not quite firmly on or with a short sheet of double foil (leaving a couple of inches uncovered). The space allows the liquid to evaporate.

2 Cook in the oven for about 2 hours, basting a couple of times. Then remove the cover and add the anchovies to the liquid, stir well (they dissolve into the sauce) and return to the oven. Increase the heat to 200°C/400°F/Gas 6 for a further 30–40 minutes, or until the lamb is tender and the sauce bubbling. Stir and taste the sauce, seasoning to taste if necessary. Carve and serve with sauce and vegetables.

Lamb Shanks with Asparagus and Mint

Looking up in my Larousse French cookbook, I turned to asparagus as I had a notion there was a famous lamb and asparagus dish from Argenteuil. I got no further than the reference to the famous vegetable, which is indeed grown in the Argenteuil region of France: 'it has no rivals', declares Larousse. Well, *au contraire*, I'm afraid it does, as here in Scotland we have some of the very best asparagus around. Sandy and Heather Pattullo (who also grow seakale) have farmed asparagus – an add-on to their cereal and potato farm at Eassie in the beautiful Vale of Strathmore between the Sidlaws and the Grampians – since 1987. Now, although there is a special asparagus-picking machine, it is usually handpicked then washed and graded (from thin 'sprue', through 'medium', 'select' then 'choice' to 'jumbo') and dispatched throughout Scotland only hours after picking. It is so tender it can also be crunched on raw – both thick and thin – and its taste is so reminiscent of raw peas it is uncanny.

This tasty dish is cooked in two stages: the long, slow casseroling of the meat one day, then on the next day, removing the fat from the chilled casserole, whizzing the sauce and roasting the asparagus. It is truly a feast; one that ought to be enjoyed at least once a week during the brief six-week asparagus season in Scotland. (Recipe continues overleaf.)

SERVES 2

3 tablespoons extra virgin olive oil
2 lamb shanks
1 onion, peeled and chopped
6–8 carrots, peeled and chopped
200ml/7 fl oz/⅓ pint red wine
200ml/7 fl oz/⅓ pint lamb stock
the juice of 1 lemon
20g/¾ oz fresh mint
450g/1 lb medium-thick asparagus, trimmed
coarse sea salt and freshly ground black pepper

1 Preheat the oven to 150°C/300°F/ Gas 2. Heat 1 tablespoon oil in a heavy, flameproof casserole then brown the shanks all over. Remove with a slotted spoon, add the onion and carrots, and fry gently for 3–4 minutes. Return the meat to the casserole, add the wine and 150ml/5 fl oz/¼ pint stock. Season then bring to the boil. Cover and place in the oven for 1½–2 hours, stirring once. Then remove and allow to cool. Refrigerate in the casserole once cold.

2 Next day, preheat the oven to 180°C/350°F/Gas 4. Scrape off any surface fat from the casserole, set the meat aside then tip the contents of the casserole into a food processor with the remaining stock (or water if you have forgotten to keep it from yesterday!). Add the lemon juice and half the mint leaves and whiz until smooth. Return this and the meat to the casserole, and cover. Cook in the oven for 30 minutes to begin reheating then increase the temperature to 200°C/ 400°F/Gas 6 and remove the casserole lid.

3 Place the asparagus on a roasting sheet, tear over the remaining mint and drizzle with the remaining oil. Season with salt and pepper. Place this sheet over the casserole as a lid and roast for a further 25–30 minutes, or until the asparagus is tender and the casserole piping hot.

4 To serve, ladle a shank and sauce on to each warmed plate (I use large, shallow soup plates), place the asparagus on top then drizzle each with the juices from the roasting tin. Serve with new potatoes.

Lamb

Swing-time at family picnic, Kirriemuir, 1958

Shetland Lamb Burgers with Noodles, Salsa and Mayonnaise Dressing

This recipe is from Marlene Hunter, who not only runs a croft with her husband on the island of Bressay in Shetland but is also cook at Bressay Primary School. It won her the title of Primary School Cook of the Year 2005 in a competition organised by Quality Meat Scotland.

SERVES 4

450g/1 lb lean lamb mince (Marlene uses Shetland heather-fed)
1 small onion, peeled and chopped
1/2 teaspoon chopped fresh rosemary
1/2 teaspoon chopped fresh mint
250g/9 oz fine egg noodles
salt and freshly ground black pepper

FOR THE SALSA

2 tomatoes, chopped
1/2 onion, finely chopped
1/4 cucumber, chopped
1 teaspoon white wine vinegar
1 teaspoon extra virgin olive oil
1 teaspoon lemon juice

FOR THE MAYONNAISE DRESSING

2 tablespoons mayonnaise
1 teaspoon wholegrain mustard

1 Mix together in a bowl the minced lamb, onion and herbs. Season lightly. Divide the mixture into four portions and shape into burgers. Chill for an hour or so if time permits. Meanwhile, preheat the oven to 200°C/400°F/Gas 6, or you can grill the burgers if you prefer.

2 Set the burgers on a wire tray over a deep roasting tin (to collect any fat) and cook in the oven for about 20 minutes. Alternatively, you can grill them under medium-high heat until thoroughly cooked.

3 To make the salsa, mix all the chopped ingredients together. Add the vinegar, oil and lemon juice. Season to taste and mix well.

4 To make the mayonnaise dressing, mix the mayonnaise and mustard together.

5 Cook the noodles in boiling water for 3 minutes and drain well. Divide the noodles among four plates, place a burger on top, spread the burger with the mayonnaise dressing and finally pile the salsa on top.

Venison and
Pheasant

I have an interesting recipe from Lapland for Moose Steaks in Moose Nose sauce beginning, 'First clean the moose's nose'. This is not one I would want to try at home, but it was in Lapland that I had my first taste of both moose and venison ('reindeer' in Finland). But I was 21 when I spent my year in northern Finland. Why on earth had I – born and bred in the land of the world's best venison – not tasted it before?

Up until perhaps the early 1980s, game (apart from rabbit and hare) was primarily the preserve of the wealthy or those who shot their own. But, hallelujah, now it is game for all, with the increasing availability of both farmed and wild. Farmed red deer is an excellent product and with a consistently good flavour and texture. In these days of obsession about health issues, it is a bonus to know that all venison is very low in fat, with an average of only 5 per cent in young deer. Because of its leanness, it must be carefully cooked: either slowly braised in plenty of liquid or fast roasted or pan-fried then allowed to rest.

Wild game also contains high proportions of healthy omega-3 fatty acids similar to those found in oily fish. If, therefore, you like to opt for free-range or organic, look no further than wild game. Deer roam the Scottish hills and glens, some of the cleanest, most unpolluted places in the world. All in all, a healthy, natural meat and one that not only appeals to our taste buds but also to the ethical environmentalist in us.

In Dundee there is a company called Highland Game, which takes in whole beasts that have been shot and gralloched (all intestines apart from liver, heart and lung removed) in the wild. After hanging, they are brought to Dundee to be butchered into easy cuts for everyday consumers to cook at home.

And so it was that I stood on the edge of Loch Rannoch with Richard Barclay, proprietor of Rannoch Smokery in Kinloch Rannoch. On a typically wet late April day, I tried to see the glory that I knew was the great peak of Schiehallion to the south west, and the hills and glens and deer. But, frankly, it was enough just to keep the hood of my cagoule up and see the edge of the loch, so grim was the weather. But, luckily, I knew the deer were there on the Innerhadden Estate in Rannoch, which the Barclay family has run for some decades. Originally sheep farmers, Richard's parents have always had to cull some 60–70 deer each year on the estate. One winter when they were snowed in, they decided that instead of allowing the beasts to be destroyed in vain, they would smoke them. And so the butchered beasts were brined in the cottage bath then smoked over a wooden box in the yard. In 1986, their first customer – Harrods – came along; not a bad catch as first customers go!

Since then the traditional method of smoking is still adhered to, but modern technology has supplanted the bath. The cold-smoked venison is made in four simple stages. The venison, butchered to Rannoch specifications at Highland Game, is brined for up to 48 hours then cold-smoked for up to 80 hours over wood chips from whisky barrels from the Craigellachie cooperage, and then sliced by hand. (They also produce 'roast-smoked venison' – hot-smoked instead of cold-smoked.)

The final stage is to lay out slices of this excellent product, toss a large salad in a bowl, cut a loaf of bread and enjoy, perhaps with a glass of good red wine (Rioja goes well). Or, if you have just been out on Loch Rannoch in your cagoule on a Scottish spring day, a cup of hot tea might be better.

Pheasant with Quince Paste and Barley Couscous

This is a really simple yet utterly delicious dish. If you cannot find barley couscous, then regular couscous is fine (the barley one is used in certain areas of Morocco where barley is more commonly grown than wheat) but the barley lends a nice earthy flavour to this gutsy game dish.

SERVES 2

2 large pheasant breasts (about 125g/4½ oz each)
50g/1¾ oz quince paste/cheese (membrillo), sliced thinly
2 tablespoons extra virgin olive oil
salt and freshly ground black pepper

FOR THE COUSCOUS

200g/7 oz barley couscous
50g/1¾ oz quince paste/cheese (membrillo)
20g/¾ oz fresh mint, chopped
10g/¼ oz fresh coriander, chopped
the juice of 2 large lemons
about 4 tablespoons extra virgin olive oil

1 Preheat the oven to 200°C/400°F/Gas 6. To make the couscous, place the barley couscous in a bowl and add 300–350ml/10–12 fl oz boiling water to cover. Cover with a lid then leave for 10 minutes. Fluff up the grains with a fork and add 1 teaspoon salt.

2 Add the remaining ingredients and enough oil to flavour. Check the seasoning. Leave the couscous to one side until it is ready to be served barely warm.

3 Using a very sharp knife, cut a slit into each pheasant breast (the thickest part) and stuff in the quince paste. Try to close up as best as possible, but don't worry if it pokes out. Heat the oil in a frying pan (preferably one that can go into the oven) and, once hot, put in the pheasant breasts. Cook for 2 minutes then carefully turn it over.

4 Place the frying pan (or transfer the breasts to a shallow oven dish) near the top of the oven for 8 minutes, or until still very slightly pink when a knife is inserted into the thickest part. Remove to a warm plate, loosely cover with foil and leave to rest for 5 minutes. Serve on a warm plate on a pile of the barley couscous and with any pan juices poured over the top.

Venison Steaks with Beetroot and Horseradish Pesto

The contrasting flavours of venison and beetroot are a match made in heaven. The pesto can be made a day or so in advance.

SERVES 4

250g/9 oz cooked beetroot, peeled and chopped
the grated zest of 1 small unwaxed orange
2 heaped teaspoons horseradish sauce
70g/2^{1}/$_{2}$ oz freshly grated Parmesan cheese
1 garlic clove, peeled and chopped
1 tablespoon chopped fresh flat-leaf parsley
about 7 tablespoons extra virgin olive oil
4 venison steaks, each about 150g/5^{1}/$_{2}$ oz
salt and freshly ground black pepper

1 Preheat the oven to 150°C/300°F/ Gas 2. To make the pesto, place the beetroot, orange zest, horseradish sauce, Parmesan, garlic and parsley in a food processor or blender and whiz briefly. Add enough oil (about 5 tablespoons) to form a thick paste. Season to taste and set aside.

2 Heat 2 tablespoons oil in a frying pan then add the steaks and season. Cook for 2 minutes, then turn and continue to cook for a further 1–2 minutes before transferring to an ovenproof plate. Place in the oven for 10 minutes then serve them on a mound of mashed potatoes and with a dollop of beetroot pesto on top.

Spiced Venison with a Wild Mushroom and Truffle Sauce

The weight of fillet from red deer can vary from around 250–400g/ 9–14 oz, but if you use a roe fillet, it will weigh only about 100g/3¹/₂ oz so you must reduce the cooking time drastically (and use a fillet per person). Whichever venison you use, remember to undercook and allow to rest for a perfect, even pinkness and tender meat.

Serve with pappardelle or soft polenta.

SERVES 3–4

1 level tablespoon whole black peppercorns
1 level tablespoon whole juniper berries
1 whole venison fillet, trimmed, about 350g/12 oz
2 tablespoons extra virgin olive oil
truffle oil, for sprinkling
sea salt and freshly ground black pepper

FOR THE SAUCE

40g/1¹/₂ oz dried porcini (ceps), rinsed
200ml/7 fl oz/¹/₃ pint dry white wine
40g/1¹/₂ oz butter
2 shallots or ¹/₂ small onion, peeled and finely chopped
2 garlic cloves, peeled and finely chopped
200g/7 oz fresh mushrooms, wiped and chopped
1 tablespoon plain flour
150ml/5 fl oz/¹/₄ pint double cream

1 Toast the peppercorns and juniper berries in a dry frying pan over high heat for about 3 minutes, shaking often, until a strong spicy smell emerges. Tip into an electric grinder – or use a mortar and pestle – and grind until coarsely ground. Brush the venison with 1 tablespoon olive oil then press in the spices. Leave on a plate somewhere cool for a couple of hours.

2 To make the sauce, soak the dried mushrooms in the wine for at least 20 minutes then strain, reserving the wine. Heat the butter in a pan and gently fry the shallots or onion and the garlic for 2–3 minutes. Add the soaked and fresh mushrooms, and stir. Cover the pan and cook for 10 minutes, or until tender.

3 Increase the heat and sprinkle over the flour. Cook for 1 minute, stirring, then add the reserved wine and the cream, stirring constantly. Bring to the boil then simmer, uncovered, for 5–10 minutes, until slightly thickened. Season to taste and set

aside. Preheat the oven to 220°C/425°F/Gas 7.

4 To cook the meat, heat the remaining olive oil in a large frying pan (preferably one that can go into the oven) and, once hot, add the venison and brown all over (4–5 minutes). Season with salt. Then transfer the pan to the oven and cook for 12 minutes per 500g/1 lb 2 oz (no longer). Remove and place on a warm plate. Cover with foil and leave to rest for 10 minutes.

5 Carve the rested meat and serve with some sauce and a few shakes of truffle oil on top.

Venison with Butternut Squash and Walnuts
Serve with good bread and a salad.

SERVES 2
1 butternut squash, cut lengthways, seeds and pith removed
2 tablespoons extra virgin olive oil
2 venison steaks, at room temperature
4 tablespoons walnut oil
25g/1 oz walnuts, chopped
salt and freshly ground black pepper

1 Preheat the oven to 200°C/400°F/ Gas 6. Cut the squash into thick wedges and place on a roasting tray. Drizzle with the olive oil and season well. Roast in the oven for 35–40 minutes, or until tender. Leave to cool a little.

2 Brush the venison all over with the walnut oil. Heat a frying pan to very hot. Season the steaks then slap them into the pan. Cook for 2 minutes on one side then turn and cook for 1–2 minutes on the other (depending on the thickness). Leave to rest somewhere warm, covered with foil, for 8–10 minutes.

3 Once the squash is cool enough to handle, scrape the flesh into a food processor. Add about 4 tablespoons walnut oil – enough to purée the squash until it has the consistency of mashed potato. Do not over purée; chunky bits are fine! Check the seasoning.

4 To serve, dollop some squash purée on to warm plates, top with the walnuts then finish with the venison steaks.

Pheasant Caesar Salad

This can be made either with a whole pheasant or with 4–6 pheasant breasts, depending on size. The main principle is not to overcook the meat so that it remains moist and succulent.

To cook a whole pheasant, roast a young bird in a hot oven for 30–40 minutes, basting often, until just done, then carve into slices. For breasts, cook as for *Pheasant with Quince Paste and Barley Couscous* on page 83.

SERVES 4

2 thick slices bread (brown or white), crusts removed, cubed
about 3 tablespoons extra virgin olive oil, plus extra for shallow frying
1 large free-range egg
1 large garlic clove, peeled and crushed
1–2 tablespoons lime or lemon juice
1 tablespoon Worcestershire sauce
4–5 anchovy fillets, snipped
1 teaspoon Dijon mustard
cos lettuce, washed and torn into large pieces
freshly cooked pheasant, sliced
25g/1 oz fresh Parmesan cheese, shaved or coarsely grated
salt and freshly ground black pepper

1 To make the croûtons, fry the bread in a little olive oil until crispy then drain on kitchen paper.

2 Place the egg in a pan of cold water and bring to the boil. Boil for 1 minute then plunge into cold water to stop the cooking. Once cool, crack into a food processor and add the garlic, 1 tablespoon citrus juice, the Worcestershire sauce, anchovies and mustard. Whiz then add enough oil to make a pourable dressing, about 3 tablespoons. Taste and season accordingly. (You might want to add more lemon or lime juice.)

3 Place the lettuce in a large, wide bowl and top with the pheasant and croûtons. Scatter over the Parmesan then drizzle over the dressing just before serving.

Black Pudding

In Arthur Herman's book *The Scottish Enlightenment*, there is a description of the Highlands in the early 1700s and the deprivation of the typical Highlander, particularly in winter. 'Highlanders often had to bleed their cattle, mixing the blood with oatmeal... Sometimes cows were bled so frequently they could barely stand.' But, thank goodness, nowadays when black pudding is made, the beast is no longer sentient.

The Kirkwall butchers, Donaldson & Sons make a wonderfully crumbly black pudding that has among the ingredients (as well as medium oatmeal) some barley (cooked pearl barley mashed down), and so both flavour and texture are wonderfully enhanced.

But possibly the most well known in Scotland is the Stornoway black pudding. And so, after a hearty Hebridean breakfast of porridge then black pudding, I went to see it being made. Charles Macleod, the butcher's shop, was opened in 1947 by the original Charley Barley. He was so-called from school days since everyone on Lewis, or so it seems, was called Macleod. After his untimely death in 1967, sons Iain and Charles took over the business and have built it up from a tiny shop to large premises. Round the back, where fabulous Hebridean lamb and venison are sold alongside the long fat rolls of various puddings (black, white, fruit), I watched Andy-the-Pudding-Man weigh out and then tip everything into huge mixing machines. When he began working here 25 years ago they were producing 300 black puddings a week, all by hand; now they produce over 3,000 and scarcely keep up with demand, which is why production is now more automated. Stornoway black pudding, made with only quality ingredients, is both earthy yet sophisticated, homely yet stylish; it is one of my very favourite foods.

Most people in the Western Isles, just like those in mainland Scotland, still confine black pudding to breakfast, but there are now more cooks serving it up for dinner. Chef Roddy Afrin of the Park Guest House in Stornoway serves it with seared scallops, caramelised peaches and a rhubarb dressing. Shona Macleod, daughter of Charles, likes it on one of her Granny Jessie's pancakes, with bacon and scallops (called 'clams' locally). Many butchers, as well as making black and white pudding, make 'fruit pudding'. At their best, they are imitations of cloutie dumpling, but in sliceable form. Ramsay of Carluke make a superb one that has the moist, pleasantly cloying texture of a perfect cloutie; and it is almost as if the characteristic outer skin from the cloutie is incorporated into the slice of pudding itself. (Andrew Ramsay's ingredients are breadcrumbs, currants, suet, sultanas, flour, milk, eggs, ginger and cinnamon.) At worst, however, some offerings of fruit pudding are too sweet, too spicy and, well, just not very nice.

Although times have changed from when most crofts made their own *marag dhubh* after a sheep was killed, nowadays fresh sheep's blood is never used. But it still has a distinctive Hebridean taste.

My next black pudding experience was on the far north-east coast of Scotland, where I watched Willie Macdonald stand over a huge trough, plunge in his hands up to his elbows, and deftly swish the beetroot porridge back and forth. Except, it was not porridge; it was black pudding and I was in Golspie, north of Dornoch, to see it made the traditional way.

Traditional means fresh blood, which is not common these days. Usually it is made from dried blood, which, according to Willie, is the work of the devil. Willie gets his ox blood still warm from the abattoir in Dingwall, ready to use for his wonderful puddings.

With the Hadden cousins, Dave, Pete and Frank, at Carnoustie swimming pool, 1958

Willie and his brother Jimmy have worked at Grants the butchers all their lives, Jimmy having started aged 12 as a message boy. Now Willie is in charge of puddings: black, white and fruit. And to start all these puddings, you need ox suet, all chopped up and finely minced in the 'bowl chopper' machine, then mixed in the trough with 30 pounds (no kilos this far north) of hand-chopped onion. 'It's no problem to chop, once you get the skins off,' Willie insists. This differentiates Grants black pudding from others, as the onions are so chunky that they add a good texture. In goes the oatmeal (stoneground, medium) and seasoning which, Willie insists, is simply salt and pepper. Or perhaps he is keen to keep something secret in case anyone decides to copy. Not that I imagine many people will be doing this at home. Especially the next stage: pouring 5 gallons of fresh blood (stirred to prevent coagulation while warm) through a fine sieve.

Then the blood is poured into the trough and mixed with dextrous arms and years of practice. The mixture now resembles a combination of beetroot porridge and thick raspberry jam, for it is a not unattractive deep crimson colour. This sloppy mixture is then scooped up and into the sausage machine where it is squooshed out ('extruded' is, I believe, the technical term) into natural ox casing for the horseshoe-shaped ring or artificial casing for the long sliceable rolls. After being hand-tied with string (Willie knows just how much room to leave for expansion to prevent bursting) they are plopped into the large steamer and simmered for 20 minutes for the rings and 1½ hours for the rolls.

Willie's final task is to delve into the steamer with a wooden spoon handle and fish out a horseshoe-shaped ring. He places it on a board and cuts it open. To paraphrase Burns, 'Oh what a glorious sicht.' I tuck in greedily with my fingers before waiting for a fork. Hot, mealy, perfectly seasoned, this is delicious. And I survived my experience without even flinching at all that blood; although I will never look at raspberry jam in quite the same way again.

Smoked Haddock with Black Pudding and Bacon

This simple recipe is divine. It is the type of dish you want to linger over, glass of red wine in hand, preferably looking out over a loch or the sea, while thanking your lucky stars for such fabulous Scottish produce. (The red wine is the obvious, but nevertheless welcome, intruder into this Arcadian scene.)

The idea came from food writer Jill Dupleix's fabulous recipe for hake with black pudding and prosciutto. Serve with a tomato salad and good bread.

SERVES 2

2 undyed smoked haddock fillets (175–200g/6–7 oz each), skinned
2 thin slices black pudding, skinned (cut very cold or it might crumble)
4 rashers traditionally cured unsmoked back bacon
extra virgin olive oil, for drizzling

1 Preheat the oven to 230°C/450°F/ Gas 8. Roll the fish so that the thin ends are tucked underneath; you want a neat little parcel. Top with the black pudding then wrap in the bacon.

2 Place on a lightly oiled baking sheet and drizzle with oil. (I don't season, as cured fish is already salted.)

3 Place the baking sheet near the top of the oven for 15 minutes, or until the fish is just cooked. Serve hot with the pan juices poured over.

Skirlie with Black Pudding

Skirlie is served here with crispy black pudding and is wonderful
served with roast lamb, chicken or on its own with a poached egg on top.

SERVES 3-4
25g/1 oz butter
3 tablespoons extra virgin olive oil
1 medium onion, finely chopped
125g/4¹/₂ oz oatmeal (half pinhead, half medium)
4–5 thick slices black pudding, skinned and cut into large dice
salt and freshly ground black pepper

1 Heat the butter and 2 tablespoons oil in a frying pan and gently fry the onion for 10 minutes, or until soft. Add the oatmeal and stir over a medium heat until toasted and crumbly, about 8–10 minutes. Season to taste.

2 Heat the remaining oil in a frying pan. Once hot, add the black pudding. Fry for 2–3 minutes, turning once, until crunchy outside and just cooked. Tip over the skirlie and serve piping hot.

BPT

Also known as a black pudding and tomato sandwich, this is one
of my all-time favourite flavour combinations. If you like a crisp roll
to hold your black pudding then opt for a crusty ciabatta or even a
chunk of baguette. But my favourite, just because it is so Scottish,
is the morning roll, bought fresh that morning. Make sure it is
soft and floury and not 'well-fired'– bliss.

SERVES 4
4 thick slices black pudding, skinned
4 morning rolls/baps (or ciabatta rolls)
tapenade (black olive paste)
8 slices tomato
sea salt

1 Fry the black pudding in a little olive oil (or grill it) until crispy outside and soft inside.

2 Open the rolls and spread one side with tapenade. Top with black pudding then tomato. Season with salt, clamp on the roll lid and devour hot.

Carnoustie Casserole with Black Pudding and Mint

My cousin-in-law Sue's sister, Jill Lamont, lives in Carnoustie, just north of Dundee. She is a great fan of casseroles so this one is for her.

Hotpot in style, this recipe has everything packed into a casserole dish, potatoes and all – and with a surprise layer of black pudding in the middle. Delicious!

SERVES 3–4

6–8 middle-neck lamb chops, trimmed
extra virgin olive oil
2 onions, peeled and sliced
700g/1 lb 9 oz potatoes, peeled and thinly sliced
1 heaped tablespoon chopped fresh mint
6–8 slices black pudding, skinned
400–500ml/14–18 fl oz/³/₄ pint hot lamb stock
a little butter
salt and freshly ground black pepper

1 Preheat the oven to 170°C/325°F/ Gas 3. Put 1 tablespoon oil into a flameproof casserole and brown the chops on both sides, then remove. Add the onions and fry for 8–10 minutes, or until golden, stirring.

2 Remove from heat then place one half of the potatoes in a layer on top of the onions. Season then add the lamb chops. Sprinkle over the mint then top with black pudding. Finally, add a layer of the potatoes. Pour over enough hot stock to come about halfway up. Dot the butter on top of the potatoes and season well.

3 Cover tightly then bake for 1¹/₄ hours. Remove the lid and continue to bake for a further 30–40 minutes, or until cooked through. Serve from the casserole with stir-fried cabbage.

Bacon

It is easy to imagine that a man who has to be up at 5.00 every morning to cure bacon might be fed up with the sight of it. On the contrary, Andrew Ramsay's face lights up as he tells me about cooking it and the very smell of it. Describing his famous Ayrshire bacon sizzling away on a griddle pan, soon becoming all crispy at the edges, he says, 'it gets you drooling before you even get to it.' And this is the man who eats his own fabulous bacon five days out of seven for breakfast; on other days he must test his sausages, for quality control purposes. He either eats his bacon simply, in a roll, or with a slice of fried fruit pudding and a runny egg. I, too, was drooling at the very thought of it.

Now, although we have endless recipes for black pudding and sausages, kippers and porridge, there is only one recipe for Scotland's bacon: the Ayrshire cure. And so when I went to Carluke to see Andrew and brother John's shop I was keen to find out why. Like the Wiltshire cure, Ayrshire bacon is brine-cured. But whereas the Wiltshire bacon sides are cured with the rind on and bones in, the Ayrshire sides have rind off and bones taken out.

The origin of the bacon in Ayrshire was as a by-product of the important dairy farming in the area with the whey being fed to the pigs, since, as Andrew explained, pigs will eat anything. (This symbiosis is, of course, not unlike Stilton cheese produced near Melton Mowbray where the pork pies are made; and Parmesan cheese near Parma ham in northern Italy.) And although this specifically Scottish cure began centuries ago, Ramsay of Carluke is the only butcher producing it traditionally by hand from start to finish on such a large scale.

But bacon starts with the pig. And it was the Ramsay brothers' great-great-grandfather who in 1857 began curing bacon from his home on a farm in Carluke, having spent his previous working life tending the Duke of Hamilton's white cattle in Hamilton. Ramsay's free-range pigs (Large White-Landrace cross) are reared in Dunning, Perthshire for them and the farmer John Neil delivers the pigs a couple of times a week to their own small abattoir beside the shop in Carluke. After the one-and-a-half hour journey, the 6-month-old pigs are slaughtered humanely and quickly in the Ramsay abattoir. This slaughterhouse is unique in Scotland as it was constructed purely to slaughter pigs. Andrew refers to them as 'lady pigs', insisting that if they were to make bacon with boars there would be a fishy taint. They are skinned then boned and trimmed then brined for about a day before being drained and matured for about two weeks. The water content of the finished bacon is 0 per cent so this is not bacon that splutters out milky liquid as it fries; rather, it crisps up nicely, giving a true lingering flavour and good firm bite.

The other distinctive feature of Ayrshire bacon is the rolling technique to produce Ayrshire middle, often just referred to as simply 'frying bacon for breakfast'. This characteristic rolling means that each slice of bacon ends up with the lean back bacon surrounded by streaky bacon: a succulent round slice with just the right ratio of gleaming white fat to lean meat.

The question of whether to choose smoked or green bacon is interesting: the sides are smoked over hardwood chips for 5–6 hours for a mild smokey flavour – or left green. Andrew's preference is for smoked and opts for either middle or streaky. The preference throughout Scotland, according to Andrew, varies regionally, with the smoked bacon first choice of the traditional fishing areas of Scotland, as they are used to the flavour of smoked fish.

As well as the famous Ayrshire bacon, Ramsay's are also producing black bacon, to a very old recipe using local ale and treacle. They also experiment with more modern cures, a current favourite being garlic and cracked pepper cured bacon, but the popular choice is always the traditional Ayrshire.

Watching the women slice and pack this, I see plenty of offcuts and trimmings from the cutting which are packed and sold, rather like cubed pancetta, for soups, stews and pasta dishes. But they are also used in Ramsay's fabulous white puddings, in addition to the other ingredients of onion, milk, oatmeal, suet and seasonings.

And so, thinking back to my question of why there has only ever been one Ayrshire bacon cure, it is obvious. Because it is so good, why change perfection? But fortunately, because bacon can be used in myriad recipes and dishes, it could never acquire the label mundane or boring.

Bacon and Mussel Chowder with Cavolo Nero

I like to use cavolo nero for this, but another young, tender kale or cabbage will do.

SERVES 3–4

500g/1 lb 2 oz mussels, well scrubbed and beards scraped off
2 tablespoons extra virgin olive oil
150g/5¹/₂ oz smoked streaky or middle bacon, diced
1 large fennel bulb, coarse outer leaves removed, sliced finely
1 leek, washed and sliced thinly
100ml/3¹/₂ fl oz dry white wine
150g/5¹/₂ oz cavolo nero, stalks stripped off, washed and shredded
salt and freshly ground black pepper

1 Discard any mussels that do not close when sharply tapped. Heat the oil in a large saucepan. Fry the bacon for about 5 minutes then add the fennel and leek, and fry for a further 5–10 minutes.

2 Stir well then add the mussels, wine, 400ml/14 fl oz hot water, and salt and pepper. Scatter the cavolo nero on top (so that it sits above the mussels and liquid; it will steam rather than boil). Increase the heat to high, cover and cook for 4 minutes, or until all the mussel shells have opened. (Reject any that remain shut.)

3 Check the seasoning and serve straight from the pan into warmed bowls, with bread.

Hebridean Chicken with Bacon

Jockie Smith-the-Pig-Man tells me why a pig's capacity to eat anything is so useful. 'They're good for gardening and they clear the woods here.' So, these dual-purpose pigs, introduced five years ago to the Dunlossit Estate on the Inner Hebridean island of Islay, are for clearing the land and also for their meat. When I drive up to the field in Billy Mcfarlane's butcher's van, there is no sign of the pigs. Until Billy-the-Butcher toots his horn and 'the girls' come running. The girls are three Middle White pigs kept for breeding purposes. They are now about 9 months old and have passed the age of slaughter (6–8 months) of their compatriots, which include Tamworth and Large Blacks. They are free to roam – just like the 70 other pigs on the machair and woods on the Islay Estate – in what is surely the most natural of all free-range environments. Here they spend their days grubbing over acres of land that is also home to deer, cattle and sheep.

Billy works with Jockie to determine how large the pigs will grow before slaughter. Billy will then have 'the girls' sent off to Paisley, the nearest abattoir, for slaughter. Then, when the carcasses return he will butcher them at his brand new cutting plant between Bowmore and Port Charlotte, ready to be sold as fresh pork or converted into sausages. Although pork has never been a traditional Scottish meat, it has always been found in crofting communities such as Islay where crofters would keep a pig for family consumption. The regeneration of pigs to the woodlands of Islay therefore makes sense, especially with their dual purpose of meat and land clearance.

Billy sells these chicken breasts ready-stuffed and wrapped in his Bowmore butcher's shop. And his are always stuffed with one-third black pudding, one-third white pudding and one-third haggis. (If using white pudding, I recommend Ritchie's of Aultbea or Ramsay of Carluke.) This is all then wrapped in dry-cured bacon (usually smoked; I prefer unsmoked for this) then cooked and served with a whisky sauce made from Islay whisky, shallots and cream. I like to serve them with nothing more than pan juices or an extra trickle of olive oil, a green vegetable and sauté potatoes. I also often use, instead of all three puddings, one or two of them, of which all combinations work well. Flexibility is the keyword here.

SERVES 2

2 large skinless chicken breasts
about 90g/3¹/₄ oz white/black pudding and haggis (or 1 or 2 of these)
4 rashers smoked or unsmoked back bacon
2 tablespoons extra virgin olive oil
salt and freshly ground black pepper

1 Preheat the oven to 200°C/400°F/ Gas 6. Place the chicken on a board and, with a small sharp knife, make a pocket along the length.

2 Combine the puddings and form two long sausages. Tuck these in the chicken breasts then cover with the flap of chicken. Season then wrap in the bacon, trying to cover as much of the chicken as possible.

3 Heat the oil in a frying pan (preferably an ovenproof one) and once hot, put in the chicken breast and sear on one side for a couple of minutes, or until browned. Then carefully turn over and place the pan in the oven for about 20 minutes, or until the chicken is just cooked. Serve at once.

Free-roaming pigs on Islay

Cock-a-leekie Risotto with Bacon

There is the most wonderful refuge from the bustle of city life on the beautiful island of Mull. Highland Cottage in Tobermory also serves some excellent food. This is my version of Chef Jo Currie's cock-a-leekie risotto. When I asked her how she had come by the idea, she said she used the cock-a-leekie recipe from my *Scots Cooking* book and integrated it into her risotto; how could I not love it?

Jo adds a generous slug of double cream at the end; I prefer to rely on the natural creaminess that comes when the outer starch on the risotto rice dissolves.

SERVES 4

75g/2³/4 oz butter
1 teaspoon extra virgin olive oil
200g/7 oz unsmoked back or middle bacon, chopped
2 skinless chicken breasts, diced
2 medium leeks, trimmed and finely sliced
300g/10¹/2 oz risotto (arborio or carnaroli) rice
150ml/5 fl oz/¹/4 pint dry white wine
1 litre/1³/4 pint hot chicken stock
10 prunes, stoned and finely chopped
55g/2 oz freshly grated Parmesan cheese
25g/1 oz flat-leaf parsley, chopped
salt

1 Melt 50g/1³/4 oz of the butter and the oil in a large pan and fry the bacon until cooked but not crispy, then remove with a slotted spoon. Add the chicken and fry, stirring, until just cooked, about 4–5 minutes, then remove with a slotted spoon.

2 Add the leeks and cook for a couple of minutes (until still vivid green but just softened), stirring. Add the rice and stir well. Once well coated in the fat, increase the heat, add the wine and bubble away for 1 minute. Then lower the heat to medium and add a ladleful of the stock. Only add the next ladleful once all the stock has been absorbed. Continue adding the stock (you might not need it all) and add salt to taste after about 10 minutes.

3 Once the rice is *al dente*, add the bacon, chicken and prunes, and stir well. Cook for 1 minute then remove from the heat. Add the Parmesan, stir well then stir in the remaining butter. Cover tightly and leave for 5 minutes.

4 Finally, stir in the parsley, check the seasoning and serve from the pan.

Haggis and Clouties

As I watched Edinburgh butcher Jonathan Crombie plop the blood-red lamb lung lobes into the bubbling water in the gargantuan boiler, it occurred to me that you need a strong stomach to watch haggis being made. Once the lungs have cooked for 2 hours, great lumps of beef fat, bacon ends and bony lamb flanks (the latter adds sweetness) are added; they all bubble away for a further hour. Then it is all minced with onions, and oatmeal is added (both medium-grade and pinhead, the latter adding that good nubbly texture). Then this is hand mixed and seasoned according to taste. And although every butcher's haggis has more or less the same ingredients, it is the seasoning that differs. All I was told at Crombie's was that it included 'all the peppers' and salt. But, as I sniffed the air, I asked, could I detect mace? An enigmatic smile and a 'Maybe' was the only response. The Crombie family's friends, the Macsweens, have a haggis factory on the outskirts of Edinburgh; their seasoning contains white pepper, mace, salt and coriander.

Once combined with lamb stock, the mixture is squished into the natural casings of beef intestine (ox bung) in the sausage machine, tied or clipped with metal clips then pricked and cooked in the steamer for 40 minutes. These days the traditional sheep's stomach is used only for the mighty 10 lb 'Chieftains', served at special ceremonial functions, such as Burns Suppers. Although it has been cooked twice by the butcher, the haggis is cooked a third time at home so all you are doing is reheating. This is another of Scotland's most natural fast foods. And if you are squeamish and reckon you couldn't possibly eat bits and pieces from inside an animal, then just think of it as a sausage. A sausage with a long and glorious CV. A good haggis – with a perfect balance of peppery spice and meaty, nutty oatmeal texture – is one of life's gastronomic treats.

Haggis sales have increased dramatically in the past few years. Macsween's, who sold some 200 tonnes a decade ago, now sell almost 700 tonnes annually. On a smaller scale, Crombie's, like many other Scottish butchers, have to make batches daily in January just to keep up with demand for Burns Night on the 25th. Like Crombie's, Macsween's have won many awards for their traditional haggis, but it was John Macsween and Sandy Crombie (Jonathan's father) who, in the early 1980s 'invented' the vegetarian haggis. Although this is packed with healthy nuts, lentils and beans, I still consider the words 'vegetarian' and 'haggis' as one oxymoron, albeit a delicious one.

Haggis is incorporated into many different dishes nowadays, from cannelloni and tartlets to stuffings and pies. One unusual stuffing I had in the Kirkwall Hotel in Orkney was delicious: an olive-oil fried bere bannock was topped with a layer of haggis and this was topped with a perfectly seared fillet steak. On the same trip, I had a fabulous pie, made by Kirkwall butchers Donaldson & Sons. Called Hagshot Pie, it is a Scotch pie case filled with haggis (theirs is very good) and topped with clapshot, Orkney's famous potato and turnip dish. Served piping hot with a dram of local malt (Highland Park or Scapa), this is food that makes sense. And I say that to counter claims that haggis should be served only with neeps and tatties and only around Burns Night.

I believe we have a wonderful 'national' dish when well made. So let's flaunt it!

'She tried some ham and a bit of the dumpling, sugared and fine, that Mistress Melon had made. And everybody praised it, as well they might, and cried for more helpings, and more cups of tea, and there were scones and pancakes and soda-cakes and cakes made with honey that everybody ate.' This description of wedding food comes from Lewis Grassic

Gibbons' *Sunset Song*. It describes the heroine Chris Guthrie's rural north-east wedding in the early twentieth century, and shows the crucial part cloutie dumplings played at special occasions. Lewis fisherman, Dods Macfarlane, told me that at weddings in the north of Lewis, he remembers there being chicken and rice broth with chicken afterwards, followed by cloutie dumpling and custard (served fried for breakfast with bacon or sliced, buttered and served cold with tea the next day). It was not everyday fare; it was the celebration cake of nowadays. When my parents grew up in Dundee there was no birthday cake; only dumpling, 'sugared and fine' and studded with sixpenny pieces wrapped in greaseproof paper. My mother tells me that her task as youngest child was to dry off the dumpling in front of the open fireplace. She would sit there on a stool for 15–20 minutes, turning the dumpling round and round until it was dried off and ready to eat.

Even when I was young, the warm, spicy smell of a cloutie dumpling would mean only one thing: a family celebration. And I was reacquainted with this alluring aroma recently as I drove along the road from Tobermory on the island of Mull to the ferry for Oban, and then home, all the while drooling with anticipation. For in the back of my car sat one of Netta MacDougall's dumplings, all plump and still hot, made especially for me to take on the 150-mile journey home. Given the enticing smell – and the nostalgia factor – I am still amazed at my willpower as I did, indeed, arrive with it whole – no telltale holes in it. Netta learned how to make cloutie dumplings from her grandmother, Janet Maclean, in the 1940s. When she asked her grandmother for the recipe, though, Janet said it was impossible, as she just added a cup of this and cup of that. (Similarly when I asked my Auntie Muriel to write down my Granny Anderson's recipe, it was also reluctantly, as she always just added 'a wee tickie of this and a wee tickie of that'!)

But Netta eventually got something down on paper and since then has made cloutie dumplings for almost everyone on Mull and beyond – she won a *Sunday Post* competition several years ago, beating off 97 rivals bearing clouties. Although Netta used to be a school-dinner cook, she now bakes and runs the tea shop at the Animal Farm near Tobermory. But whenever there is a family gathering (she has three children and seven grandchildren), she makes a dumpling; although just before I arrived, she had made 18 in one weekend. When I asked why, she simply said, 'People like them', which was a good enough reason for me.

And, having watched her remove the magnificently bulging cloutie from the bubbling water, and nimbly remove the string and then the clout (cloth), and invert it on to a warm plate to dry off in the oven, I could not help but wonder if Netta had realised yet that I, too, like them. ('Like' being too mild a word in fact.) Thankfully she did, as testified by that alluring aroma of childhood (it was still warm four hours later) on my long drive home.

Dolina Macdonald was born and brought up on the island of Tiree. I was lucky enough to try her cloutie dumpling during a visit there and it, too, was one of the best I have tasted: moist, rich and fruity, and with the characteristic skin (beware skinless clouties, as they are not authentic). I had some of Dolina's dumpling for breakfast in the Scarinish Hotel in Tiree with black pudding and eggs, and it was exquisite. However, the most common way of eating cloutie dumpling on Tiree (and this is not as common on nearby Mull or in Dundee), is cold, cut into slices then into fingers like a fruit cake. It is usually spread with butter, the latter being very important to the crofting communities that still thrive there. Dolina well remembers her arm aching as she had to churn butter on their croft. Freshly churned butter on a slice of cloutie on Tiree is another example of certain foods being the perfect embodiment of the place. And, since my visit, I have quite taken to eating it cold, not always daintily sliced or even with butter; sometimes, I am ashamed to say, torn off in inelegant clumps. The simplest foods taste best.

Haggis Lasagne

Serve with salad and a bottle of gutsy red wine; at wine pairings, haggis often comes out best with an Australian Shiraz. But for this particular dish, Valvona & Crolla – Scotland's finest Italian deli and wine merchant – recommend an Aglianico from Campania. *Salute!*

SERVES 6

1 large haggis, about 900g/2 lb
about 250g/9 oz no pre-cook lasagne
3–4 large, ripe tomatoes, sliced
salt and freshly ground black pepper

FOR THE SAUCE

40g/1¹/₂ oz butter
40g/1¹/₂ oz plain flour
500ml/18 fl oz milk
3 tablespoons freshly grated
    Parmesan cheese
extra virgin olive oil, for drizzling

1 Preheat the oven to 180°C/350°F/ Gas 4. Cut open the haggis and crumble with your fingers. Scatter some over the base of a buttered lasagne dish. Top with a third of the lasagne sheets then top with more haggis. Add a layer of tomatoes and season well, then cover with lasagne and the remaining haggis. Finish with the remaining lasagne.

2 To make the sauce, melt the butter and stir in the flour to form a roux. Gradually add the milk, stirring or whisking to form a sauce. Stir for 4–5 minutes then season to taste. Pour this over the lasagne, top with the cheese and a drizzle of oil.

3 Bake, uncovered, for 50–55 minutes, or until golden and the lasagne is soft. (Check with the tip of a knife.) Rest for 10 minutes or so before cutting.

Sue's Haggis Rolls

When we organised a family picnic up Glen Clova (north of Dundee) for 41 members of our family, from my hill-climbing Uncle Frank – the oldest, aged 87 – to the youngest, Kirsty Henderson aged 15, we, the seven 'middle-aged' cousins (in years, not mentality!) all took picnics and, as always, vastly over-catered. But one of the family favourites was Sue Hadden's haggis rolls, which were eaten hot on the journey there and also devoured cold up the Glen.

SERVES 4

1 medium haggis
4 crusty rolls or half-baguettes, split
2 tomatoes, sliced (optional)

1 Heat the haggis according to the butcher's instructions (or wrap in foil and heat in a medium oven for about 40 minutes).

2 Divide the haggis among the rolls, packing in generously. Tuck in tomato slices, if you like. Wrap at once in foil then take on a picnic to eat warm or cold, but freshly filled is best.

Stein Inn Haggis Toastie

Skye's oldest Inn, Stein Inn in Waternish (1790), is home to great pub food, including Haggis Toastie, local langoustines and oatmeal scallops.

SERVES 4

1 small haggis
300ml/10 fl oz dark beer
8 slices of brown bread, buttered
butter
salt and freshly ground black pepper

1 Heat the haggis according to the butcher's instructions (or wrap in foil and heat in a medium oven for about 40 minutes). Once piping hot, open up the haggis and tip into a bowl.

Add the beer and seasoning to taste. The mixture should not be too soggy. Leave for a couple of minutes for the oats in the haggis to absorb the beer and firm up.

2 Spread four slices of buttered bread thickly with the haggis mixture then make a sandwich with the other slice. Place in a toastie machine and cook until toasted (or grill on one side then carefully turn and grill the other until golden). (Any leftover haggis can be refrigerated then reheated later.)

Haggis in Pitta with Tzatsiki

I know, how weird does this sound, but trust me: it is sublime. The combination is not dissimilar to one of those lightly spiced lamb dishes served with garlicky tzatsiki in Greece. But do not take my word for it – try it. It is a revelation. Different, yes; daft, most certainly not.

SERVES 4
1 medium haggis
4 pitta breads, toasted until warm and puffy
salt and freshly ground black pepper
FOR THE TZATSIKI
1 medium cucumber, wiped, ends removed
200ml/7 fl oz Greek yogurt
1 tablespoon extra virgin olive oil
the juice of $1/2$ lemon
2 heaped tablespoons chopped fresh mint
1 fat garlic clove, peeled and crushed

1 To make the tzatsiki, grate the cucumber, unpeeled, and place the grated flesh in a colander over a bowl. Sprinkle with 2 teaspoons salt, and leave for about an hour.

2 Using your hands, squeeze out all the liquid then pat dry with kitchen paper. Place in a bowl with the remaining ingredients and stir to combine. Add pepper to taste.

3 Heat the haggis according to the butcher's instructions (or wrap in foil and heat in a medium oven for about 40 minutes).

4 Split the warm pitta breads then fill with a couple of spoonfuls of haggis. Top with a couple of spoonfuls of tzatsiki. Devour hot and messily.

Cloutie Dumpling

This recipe is based on my Granny Anderson's, made so often by my Auntie Muriel. But I have incorporated elements from the recipes of both Netta from Mull and Dolina from Tiree. The result, I think, is excellent: it is moist, fruity, dark and with just enough spice.

If you want to add coins, wrap five-pence pieces or charms in waxed or greaseproof paper and add to the mixture.

SERVES 12

450g/1 lb self-raising flour, sifted
200g/7 oz golden caster sugar
1 level teaspoon ground cinnamon
1 heaped teaspoon mixed spice
125g/4^1/$_2$ oz shredded suet
450g/1 lb mixed dried fruit (sultanas, currants, raisins)
^{1}/$_2$ teaspoon bicarbonate of soda
a pinch of salt
2 tablespoons black treacle
about 450ml/16 fl oz full-cream milk
flour and caster sugar, to sprinkle

1 Mix the flour, sugar, cinnamon, mixed spice, suet, dried fruit and bicarbonate of soda together in a bowl. Add the salt, then drizzle over the treacle. Add enough milk to make a soft mixture of a stiff yet dropping consistency.

2 Dip a pudding cloth (or large tea towel) into boiling water to scald, then drain well (I use rubber gloves to squeeze it dry) and lay out flat on a board. Sprinkle with flour and then sugar (I use my flour and sugar shakers); you want an even – but not thick – sprinkling. (This forms the characteristic skin.)

3 Now (and this is Netta's trick), put the cloth over a bowl and let it drop gently in (this keeps the shape much better). Spoon the mixture into the cloth then draw up the corners and tie securely with string, allowing a little room for expansion.

4 Place the cloutie on a heatproof plate in the bottom of a large saucepan. Top up with boiling water to just about cover the pudding (it must come at least three-quarters up the side of the pudding) then cover with a lid and simmer gently for about 3^1/$_2$ hours. Check the water level occasionally and top up if necessary.

(You should continually hear the reassuring, gentle shuddering sound of the plate on the bottom of the pan for the entire duration of cooking.)

5 Preheat the oven to 180°C/350°F/ Gas 4. Wearing rubber gloves, remove the pudding from the pan and dip briefly into a bowl of cold water (no more than 10 seconds) so that the skin does not stick to the cloth. Cut the string, untie the cloth and invert the dumpling on to a warmed ovenproof plate.

6 Place in the oven for 10–15 minutes to dry off the skin: it should feel a little less sticky. Sprinkle with caster sugar and serve hot with custard.

Mum as a toddler with Granny and Grandpa Ward and her sisters, Broughty Ferry picnic, 1925

Cloutie Dumpling Ice Cream

There is a similar recipe for Selkirk Bannock Ice Cream, which is made by Borders ice cream makers, Mackays of Eyemouth. They mix broken-up bannock from Dalgetty's of Galashiels into the ice cream with some toffee sauce and a hint of cinnamon. Theirs is a winner and is served by Kelso Chef Gary Moore with his famous Selkirk bannock bread and butter pudding, which has become a Borders classic.
To make it yourself, simply substitute the cloutie dumpling with bannock and add a hint of cinnamon.

SERVES 6

300ml/10 fl oz/^{1}/$_2$ pint double cream
200g/7 oz condensed milk
1 tablespoon malt whisky
200g/7 oz cloutie dumpling, without skin

1 Whip the cream to soft peaks, then gently fold in the milk and whisky. Once combined, tip into a freezer container and freeze for about 3 hours, whisking a couple of times.

2 Tear off clumps of cloutie (do not crumble into small crumbs) and gently stir in. Refreeze until firm.

3 Serve with hot butterscotch sauce.

Potatoes

Anyone who thinks to make a scarecrow out of CDs has to be more than a little enterprising. And Hilary Cochran is most certainly that. She has built up her farm shop, at Knowes Farm near East Linton in East Lothian, from a little one selling only eggs and potatoes some 30 years ago to a thriving rural business that has, however, managed to keep its appeal. Husband Peter, whose father began farming here in 1947, explains that the CDs on the scarecrows glint for miles. I then ask the obvious question, and, yes, it works with all CDs, whether Barry Manilow or Madonna!

So, having visited the farm shop (with its fabulous local bacon, Argyll venison, Biggar ice cream, Haddington cheese and home-grown vegetables), I was off to the tattie fields.

Long dreels (rows) of potatoes stretch into the distance on their 360-acre arable farm, some with the shaws (the green part of the plant) still growing. Earlies such as Epicure were originally grown on this farm until the late 1960s after which only maincrop potatoes were grown. The reason for stopping was simple: on this east coast of Scotland, the season was always some three weeks after Ayrshire's earlies and so there was less demand. (Ayrshire, on the west coast, is ahead of the east coast, with the warming influence of the Gulf Stream.) But about the time the farm shop opened, the Cochrans began earlies again, since the climate and soil here are so ideal. (The proximity to the sea means there are seldom bitter frosts.) And because there were only 'tasteless Jerseys' or imported potatoes the Cochrans could see a market, albeit a niche one, for earlies. They now pride themselves in growing these old-fashioned, slower-growing, lower-yielding but better-flavoured varieties.

Many people do not realise that only maincrop potatoes can be stored for a long time. Earlies, because of their 'fluffy' skin do not last much longer than about a week. Cold storage changes all potatoes and Hilary is suspicious of those who refrigerate tatties, which alters the sugar content and makes them taste sweet and inferior. Maincrop potatoes are left for at least three weeks without the shaws on, during which time the skin sets. An easy test of an early potato is to rub the skin: if you can rub it off, it is probably an early.

As we strolled up and down the dreels in glorious July sunshine (the earlies season is from the end of June until August, having been planted in March; maincrop are harvested from August until early October), Peter dug up samples for me to take home. There were Epicures (round, slightly dimpled and waxy – the variety that made Ayrshire famous for earlies) and red- and white-skinned Duke of Yorks (oval-shaped and drier, also known as Midlothian Early) and Sharpe's Express (another drier potato, oval, yellowish in colour). As well as these earlies, I also had some Charlottes (a modern waxy potato) and Pink Fir Apples. Dunbar Standards (like Pink Firs, also maincrop) are also being trialled and indeed they were bred on the neighbouring farm around 1936.

Once home, I rubbed the fluffy skins off, boiled them, then served some with toasted oatmeal, some topped with melted local Haddington Camembert-like cheese and some *au naturel* with nothing more than a dod of butter. Exquisite as these first two are, there is nothing quite as delicious as a simple bowl of Scottish earlies, boiled or steamed and served as they are. Even enterprising Hilary is inclined to agree on simplicity being the best treatment for such perfect little tubers.

Sue with Dad and Carol at Reekie Linn, near Alyth, 1960

Oatmeal Tatties
If you cannot find pinhead oatmeal, medium oatmeal will do.

SERVES 3–4
about 500g/1 lb 2 oz earlies, lightly scrubbed
2–3 tablespoons pinhead oatmeal
40g/1¹/₂ oz butter

1 Cook the potatoes until just tender (boiled or steamed) then drain well.

2 Meanwhile, toast the oatmeal under a grill until you can just begin to smell its nutty aroma. Add the butter to the potatoes then sprinkle over the toasted oatmeal. Toss gently to coat then serve piping hot.

Potatoes

Clapshot Soup with Haggis Croûtons

Instead of making this from scratch, I have also liquidised leftover clapshot with some good stock; and don't forget plenty of black pepper.

SERVES 4

1 litre/1¾ pints chicken stock
500g/1 lb 2 oz potatoes, peeled and chopped
500g/1 lb 2 oz turnip (swede), peeled and chopped
1 large carrot, peeled and chopped
1 onion, peeled and chopped
1 thin French stick
extra virgin olive oil, for brushing
1 small haggis
salt and freshly ground black pepper

1 Bring the stock to the boil in a large saucepan then add the vegetables and some salt and pepper. Once at boiling point, lower to a simmer, cover and cook for about 25 minutes, or until tender, then liquidise and check the seasoning. Meanwhile, preheat the oven to 180°C/350°F/Gas 4.

2 To make the croûtons, slice a thin French stick, place the slices on a baking tray and brush lightly with oil. Bake for about 10 minutes, or until golden. Heat a small haggis according to the butcher's instructions (or wrap in foil and heat in a medium oven for about 40 minutes), then scoop some on to a croûton.

3 Ladle the soup into warm bowls and top with a couple of haggis croûtons.

Clapshot

This wonderful yet simple dish is from Orkney, and during a visit there I was lucky enough to try various versions. Sometimes the turnip is cooked in milk, which makes it even creamier; but I advise you to use a very deep saucepan and keep the heat low once it has come to the boil, otherwise the milk boils over easily. Sometimes a peeled, chopped onion is added to the potatoes as they cook, for extra flavour. But this one here is the basic recipe, using plenty of good butter; Orkney's dairy produce is superb and the local butter, milk, cream and cheese abundant.

Elsewhere in the UK, it is easy for us to think that a turnip is a turnip. Well, not on Orkney. There, they are very particular about using winter turnips (also known as neeps in Scotland) if possible, as they are drier and so the clapshot is not watery. Also, in order to have as much of the turnip's inherent sweetness, the best are those that have been in the ground through a hard frost. A final tip to make this dish truly Orcadian is to use a heavy hand with the pepper. Locals love it really peppery.

SERVES 4–6

500g/1 lb 2 oz potatoes (peeled weight), peeled and cut up
500g/1 lb 2 oz turnip (swede) (peeled weight), peeled and cut up
70g/2^{1}/$_{2}$ oz butter
1–2 tablespoons chopped chives (optional)
salt and freshly ground black pepper

1 Cook the vegetables in boiling water until tender (I bring them to the boil in cold salted water then boil, covered, for 15–20 minutes, depending on size), then drain. Return them to the pan, cover them and put over a very low heat. Shake the pan to dry them off completely.

2 Mash with the butter, then add salt and pepper to taste and the chives, if using. Serve piping hot.

Macaroon Bars

Macaroon bars seem to be a peculiarly Scottish sweet. Let's face it, who, apart from the Scots with our renowned sweet tooth, would look at a leftover boiled potato and decide to mix it with sugar then dip it in chocolate and coconut? For this is the old-fashioned – and undeniably the best – way of making these delicious sweets, which used to rival tablet in popularity at church fairs or garden fêtes. Nowadays, commercial producers make them from sugar mixed with fondant and glucose.

This recipe is from the kitchen of the wonderful Mary Coghill, octogenarian of Brora, who has made these for many years for her family. One rainy day in Sutherland, her daughter Dawn Powell and I helped her make them and wolfed down the results with many cups of tea.

MAKES 24–30

1 medium potato (preferably floury), peeled and boiled (boiled weight 75g/2³/₄ oz)
400–450g/14 oz–1 lb icing sugar (use white, not golden icing sugar, for these)
200–250g/7–9 oz quality chocolate (I like half milk, half dark)
125–150g/4¹/₂–5¹/₂ oz desiccated coconut

1 Lightly butter a rectangular tin (about 23 x 18cm/9 x 7 in). Boil the potato in unsalted water then drain and thoroughly dry. Place this very dry potato in a food mixer (not a food processor) and begin to mix with the flat beaters. Very gradually start adding unsieved icing sugar a little at a time. Continue to add the sugar until the correct consistency is achieved: the paste should be smooth and stiff. (You can of course do this by hand but it is arduous.)

2 Tip into the prepared tin and smooth out. Chill for an hour or so (or pop into the freezer for about 20 minutes) until hard.

3 Meanwhile, melt the chocolate (Mary does this in a shallow bowl for easy dipping). Toast the coconut by dry-frying, in batches, in a frying pan. Tip the coconut on to a large plate.

4 Cut and separate the set mixture into bars (working quickly or inveigling others into getting their sleeves up and helping), and dip each bar into the chocolate (I use two forks). Now dip the bars into the coconut (again using two forks), then place on a sheet of greaseproof paper on a board to harden.

Kale

Mike Callender surveys his four 100-metre long beds of organic kale and explains why – unlike cabbages – the slugs ignore kale. 'Too much of a climb up the long stem, I suppose.' I had expected some intricate agricultural fact dating back to the time before chemicals were doused over every growing thing, but for Mike it is simple. And, of course, with organic food it often is, although it is also incredibly hard work. Mike and his partner Fu Aykroyd's company, East Coast Organics (whence cometh my weekly organic box), has been expanding so much over the nine years they have farmed and delivered that they now have over 1,000 customers. But, apart from obvious exceptions such as bananas and delicate herbs in the winter, over 80 per cent of the goods packed into the boxes is theirs. Right alongside the kale beds I spotted the hen houses, where a flock of happy organic hens pecked around under the bright winter sun. Not so happy the other night, Mike told me, when the foxes got 30 of them. There are downsides to this free-range lifestyle.

Mike farms four types of kale: the classic curly kale, Red Russian kale, purple curly kale and cavolo nero. But it is the basic curly kale that is most widely used; from Brazil where it is crisply fried and served with the bean and meat dish *feijoada*, to Ostfriesland in north Germany where it is cooked with pork, sausages and oatmeal or groats to produce *Grunkohl*, a dish eaten with almost religious fervour – and washed down with litres of schnapps.

In Scotland we have known and loved curly kale for centuries. In most regions, this hardy winter vegetable was grown, not only for its ability to withstand severe cold and frost but also because, as is now recognised, it is a superstar nutritionally, packed with calcium, potassium, iron, vitamins A and C, and high in fibre. So commonplace was it as a vegetable, the word 'kail' (the Scots spelling) had other meanings. To be asked to take kail was an invitation for a meal. The kail-yard was the term for the kitchen garden where vegetables were grown. F. Marian McNeill, in her description of a Scottish kitchen in a 'but-and-ben' (two-roomed cottage) or croft, wrote of the kail-pot: a round iron pot with three legs to stand over the peat fire. This and the iron girdle (griddle) were the two most basic pieces of cooking equipment. In the kail-pot, as well as porridge, the midday broth was made. My mother remembers broth referred to in her childhood as simply kail because of the vegetable in the soup.

Apart from broths, brose (oatmeal-based broths) and soups, kail was served on its own, with butter and milk added when available. Dr Samuel Johnson remarked in his *A Journey to the Western Islands of Scotland* that 'when they (the Scots) had not kail, they probably had nothing'. Kail brose was eaten in some regions in a way similar to the ritual of porridge eating that my parents grew up with, milk and porridge being in separate bowls. For the brose, toasted oatmeal was placed in a bowl with salt, then a ladleful of boiling beef broth added and puréed kail served separately. A spoonful of kail was dipped into the broth and the two eaten together. At the onset of spring, nettles would be substituted in the brose recipe.

Now the memory of gargantuan platters containing fatty pork sausage, *kassler* and speck perched on piles of slimy, brownish-green kale no longer fills me with nausea, for I now appreciate the problem was not with the ingredients *per se* but the cooking. Broken down into singular components, this could be a fine dish, but cooked – as the Ostfriesland kale was – for 2–3 hours, the root of the problem was obvious.

These days I cook kale for the minimum of time, whether crisply stir-fried with garlic and olive oil or lightly braised with tomatoes and peanut butter for a creamy treat to serve with roast chicken. Kale works well with bacon, sausages, beans, smoked fish, cheese and root vegetables.

Sue and cousin Dave at Carnoustie, 1957

Cheese and Kale Risotto

I have used both green and purple kale successfully for this dish. You can decrease the amount of Parmesan if you like, but I love the contrast of the creamy, salty cheese and the slightly bitter kale.

SERVES 3–4

100g/3¹/₂ oz smoked back bacon, chopped
200g/7 oz kale, stalks stripped off, washed and shredded
50g/1³/₄ oz butter
1 medium onion, peeled and chopped
1 celery stick, chopped
250g/9 oz arborio or carnaroli rice
100ml/3¹/₂ fl oz white wine
about 700ml/1¹/₄ pints hot chicken stock
75g/2³/₄ oz freshly grated Parmesan cheese
salt

1 Fry the bacon in a hot frying pan until golden, then add the kale. Stir well then cover. Reduce the heat and allow to 'steam' for 3–4 minutes, or until the kale is just tender. Set the pan aside.

2 Heat half the butter in a large saucepan, and gently fry the onion and celery until soft. Add the rice. Increase the heat, stir well then add the wine and bubble for a minute or so. Reduce the heat to medium and add the stock, a ladleful at a time, only adding more liquid when the previous ladleful has been absorbed.

3 After 15 minutes of cooking time tip in the bacon and kale, and add salt to taste. Continue cooking until the rice is *al dente*, a further 3–5 minutes. (You may not need all the stock.)

4 Turn off the heat, stir in the cheese, then, once the cheese is incorporated, add the remaining butter. Stir well, put the lid on and allow to stand for a few minutes before serving straight from the pan.

Kale Soup with Arbroath Smokies

This delicious soup retains a vivid green colour since you add in fresh kale towards the end. A traditional kail brose would have used beef stock: classically it was made by boiling an ox head, cow heel or marrow bone to make good fatty stock, then the kale was cooked in this, with some toasted oatmeal stirred in towards the end to thicken and flavour. Lady Clark of Tillypronie advocated a half teacupful of warmed cream just before serving. And although this might sound extravagant, it is not impossible that some cottages and crofts would have cream to spare after their cottage cheese – crowdie – was made.

If you cannot get your hands on smokies, lightly poach some undyed smoked haddock and use that instead.

SERVES 4

300g/10$^{1/2}$ oz kale, stalks stripped off, washed and roughly chopped
1.2 litre/2 pints hot chicken stock
1 medium onion, peeled and chopped
50g/1$^{3/4}$ oz medium oatmeal
1 pair of Arbroath Smokies, flesh flaked and checked for bones
Dijon mustard, to taste
extra virgin olive oil
salt and freshly ground black pepper

1 Place about three-quarters of the kale in a large pan with the hot stock and onion. Bring to the boil then cover and cook over a medium heat, stirring once, for 10 minutes, or until the kale is just tender.

2 Meanwhile, place the oatmeal on a sheet of foil and place under a preheated grill for 3–4 minutes, shaking often to prevent burning, until toasted and pale golden.

3 Tip the soup into a blender or liquidiser with the remaining kale, and blend. (You will need to do this in two batches.)

4 Return to the pan and gradually stir in the oatmeal as you cook over a medium heat. Add 1 level teaspoon salt and plenty of freshly milled pepper. Cook, stirring to avoid lumps, for 4–5 minutes, or until thickened. Meanwhile, warm the fish until barely warm (a short twirl in the microwave is easiest, or 10 minutes in a medium oven).

5 Add 1 heaped teaspoon mustard, then stir and check the seasoning, adding more mustard if you like. Ladle into warmed bowls, top with flaked smokies and drizzle with oil just before serving.

Bean, Kale and Sausage Crusty Hotpot

A kind of Scottish cassoulet, but with a nod towards the fabulous Brazilian *feijoada*, which is a hearty bean, pork and beef dish served with crisply fried shredded kale on the side, with orange slices and *farofa*, toasted cassava flour. I happen to love both French and Brazilian dishes, and so my one has elements of both: sausages as well as black pudding, butter beans (Scotland's favourite bean) and kale. I also cheat and use tinned beans, which makes this far less lengthy to make.

You can substitute white pudding for the black on top if the white pudding is, rather like Ramsay of Carluke's, a sliceable, firm one rather than a scoopable crumbly one. Serve with a salad of floppy green lettuce, dressed in a mustardy vinaigrette.

SERVES 4–6

1 tablespoon extra virgin olive oil
100g/3^1/$_2$ oz streaky bacon, diced
1 onion, peeled and chopped
2 garlic cloves, peeled and chopped
2 celery sticks, chopped
about 400g/14 oz best sausages (pork or beef)
200g/7 oz kale, stalks stripped off, washed and shredded
400g/14 oz chopped tomatoes
2 x 400g/14 oz butter beans, drained
100ml/3^1/$_2$ fl oz red wine
4–6 slices black pudding (or sliceable white pudding)
50g/1^3/$_4$ oz fresh brown breadcrumbs
50g/1^3/$_4$ oz freshly grated Parmesan cheese
salt and freshly ground black pepper

1 Preheat the oven to 200°C/400°F/ Gas 6. Heat the oil in a large flameproof casserole and fry the bacon for a couple of minutes, or until the fat runs, then add the onion, garlic and celery. Fry for 2–3 minutes then add the sausages and brown them all over.

2 Add the kale and fry for a couple of minutes, stirring, until just wilted.

Add the tomatoes, beans and red wine, and bring to the boil. Season and remove from the heat. Place the black (or white) pudding on top. Mix the bread and cheese, and sprinkle all over the top, patting down gently.

3 Bake uncovered for 40–45 minutes, or until crusty on top and piping hot underneath.

Rumbledethumps

This is one of my mother's favourite dishes, although she uses cabbage instead of kale. The etymology of this Borders dish is simple: 'rumbled' means mashed or stirred together, and 'thumped' means pounded together. This is tasty with sausages, lamb chops or roast chicken.

SERVES 6

650–700g/1 lb 7oz–1 lb 9 oz potatoes, peeled and chopped
450–500g/1 lb–1 lb 2 oz turnip (swede), peeled and chopped
200g/7 oz kale, stalks stripped off, washed and shredded
75g/2³/₄ oz butter
50g/1³/₄ oz mature farmhouse Cheddar, grated
salt and freshly ground black pepper

1 Preheat the oven to 180°C/350°F/ Gas 4. Cook the potatoes and turnip in boiling salted water until tender, then drain thoroughly.

2 Cook the kale by sautéing in the butter over a medium heat for 4–5 minutes, until wilted but still vivid green.

3 Tip the kale and all the butter into the potato pan and mash everything together, season to taste with plenty of salt and freshly milled black pepper. Tip into an ovenproof dish. Sprinkle over the cheese and bake uncovered for about 30 minutes, or until golden brown and piping hot.

Sue with Carol and Mum near Oban, 1963

Kale

Seakale with Parmesan

The old-fashioned vegetable, seakale, is a crucifer that traditionally grew close to the sea in sand and shingle. Having been common as a wild vegetable around the coasts of the UK, including southern Scotland, it was introduced as a cultivated vegetable to kitchen gardens in the early eighteenth century and, according to Sandy Patullo of Eassie Farm, Glamis, Angus, it was found in most walled gardens of the Big Houses in Scotland during the nineteenth century. It is in season in the early spring. I am lucky enough to be able to buy seakale of superb quality from the Patullos, although their main seasonal crop is asparagus.

Seakale is usually steamed or boiled until just tender and served with a butter-based sauce. I prefer a dousing of best olive oil and a sprinkling of Parmesan.

SERVES 2–3

225g/8 oz seakale

2 tablespoons extra virgin olive oil

2 tablespoons coarsely grated Parmesan cheese

1 Trim off the ends of the seakale stalks and rinse well. To cook, either steam for about 4 minutes or pop into boiling water (I use a wide, deep frying pan instead of a tall saucepan) and boil for about 4 minutes, or until just tender. Drain then thoroughly pat dry in a tea towel.

2 Place in a hot serving dish and drizzle over the oil, then sprinkle with the cheese. Serve at once.

Seaweed

As I stroll down to Auchmithie beach one chilly spring day with local cook and restaurateur Margaret Horn, she tells me about childhood summers of jam pieces and pepper dulse. It was on the beach, a short walk down from the tiny clifftop village of Auchmithie, on the north-east coast, that she spent her days playing, picking and eating seaweed, and, during the month of May, watching the boys collect gulls' eggs from the cliffs. Another local, George Cargill, then joins us and he tells me how he used to be lowered from the top of the cliff with a rope down to the gulls' nests and then take a clutch home for tea. Margaret says they make the very best omelette.

But it is not the gulls' eggs we are here to see, nor the limpets we step over, while Margaret tells me they used to eat these shellfish stewed with onion and potato; nor even to talk of Auchmithie's fascinating history (it was first mentioned in the Chartulary of Arbroath in 1434) or its place in literature, as 'Mussel-crag', beside the town of 'Fairport' (Arbroath), the setting of Sir Walter Scott's 1816 novel, *The Antiquary*. No, we were here for the seaweed, that lesser known accompaniment to the great Scottish jam sandwich!

As I struggle across the wet pebbles and rocks, Margaret suddenly cries 'Dulse!' or 'Tangles!' or 'Carragheen!' and I follow, as quickly as possible, given the slippiness (and my pathetically city – minus the slicker – ways). My hands turn to white as the raw east-coast haar envelops us and I struggle to hold open the various carrier bags for Margaret to drop in the specific seaweeds. Dulse (*Palmaria palmata*) is abundant and so there is a large bag of this, ready to be converted into soup. Margaret tells me about the traditional way of eating dulse at home, which was to 'roast' it by wrapping it around a red-hot poker, holding it over a fire then sprinkling with vinegar and devouring at once, while the taste of the sea mingles with that wonderfully salty iodine flavour. There is also plenty of kelp (*Laminaria digitata*), known in Scotland as 'tangles', and this Margaret wraps around haddock then poaches until just done so that the seaweed flavour is imparted delicately into the fish. The carragheen (*Chondrus crispus*), less abundant on Auchmithie's beach, is thrust into a small bag. Margaret will make a wobbly blancmange-like milk pudding to be eaten with rhubarb, later on. Pepper dulse (*Laurencia pinnatifida*), the one Margaret and George remember from childhood as the 'hors d'oeuvre' to their jam sandwich, has the most sublime taste. It is spicy, peppery and exotic all at once; easy to see why this was often used as a condiment. (I could have also sworn that there was a hint of truffle oil as I tasted it; but then I was fast becoming hypothermic and my senses were slowly shutting down – perhaps I was approaching nirvana.) It is also by no means scarce, but, because it is so easy to eat, none goes into the bag that brisk April morning; all goes into the mouth. But, should you be rather more restrained than I, then it can be used in similar ways to dulse. Interestingly, it is also known as 'poor man's tobacco' and is chewed until the wonderfully pungent flavour is released. (Was it tobacco and not truffle I tasted in my hypothermic state?)

Sloke or Slouk (*Porphyra umbilicalis*), also known as nori in Japan and laver in Wales, is less common on Margaret's beach, but it was traditionally converted into soup all over the Hebrides and on the island of Barra made into 'Slokan', a dish of the pulped seaweed mixed with butter and seasoning then served piping hot atop a mound of mashed potatoes and often some fried onions.

As we began slowly ambling up the hill towards Margaret's famous restaurant, the But 'n' Ben, I dreamed of a hot drink, both to sip and also to get my numb hands around. Piping hot coffee and a slab of Margaret's wonderful cinnamon nablab did the trick to restore white fingers to normality, and so I was ready to be shown not only the traditional hot-poker roasting method for dulse but also the modern method: in the microwave. The noise made by a small dish of dulse cooking for mere seconds in the microwave is the same as the noise a piece of foil inadvertently left in a bowl of melting chocolate makes when being microwaved: an alarmingly loud, sizzling crackle. This is surely to do with the high mineral content of seaweed. Dulse, for example, contains one of the highest concentrations of iron in any foodstuff. And all seaweeds are a rich source of antioxidants such as beta-carotene and the vitamins B_1, B_2 and B_{12}. In short, it is a wonder-food.

And there is something else about seaweed that has, thus far, never been proven, but is glaringly obvious as one looks around the more elderly locals of Auchmithie who have eaten seaweed all their lives: there is hardly a grey or white hair between them. Is there therefore something in the seaweed that is the secret of eternal youth? Margaret herself is *d'un certain age*, with teenage grandchildren, and yet looks at least 10 years younger. Seaweed is exceedingly healthy, tasty, more versatile than merely as an adjunct to a jam piece – and it is free; what better recommendation can there be for Scots to eat more of it?

Fresh Dulse Soup
When picking wild seaweed, ensure it is from clean water and that there is not a sewage plant lurking just around the bay!

SERVES 6

about 200g/7 oz freshly picked dulse, well washed
4 large potatoes, peeled and chopped
2 onions, peeled and chopped
salt and freshly ground black pepper
rough oatcakes, to serve

1 Place the dulse, potatoes and onions in a large saucepan and cover with water. Bring to the boil then simmer for about 10 minutes, or until the potatoes are tender.

2 Liquidise and add salt and pepper to taste. Crumble some rough oatcakes over the top just before serving.

Dulse and Mint Tapenade

Serve this smeared on little squares of toast as canapés to serve with champagne; make the toast round and you can call them crostini to serve with prosecco.

MAKES ENOUGH FOR 1 JAR

10g/¼ oz dried dulse, washed then soaked in warm water for
    10 minutes and drained
100g/3½ oz black olives (pitted weight)
1 heaped tablespoon capers (soaked well if salted)
1 garlic clove, peeled and chopped
1 heaped tablespoon fresh mint
juice of 1 small lemon
3–4 tablespoons extra virgin olive oil
salt and freshly ground black pepper

1 Place the drained dulse in a small food processor with the olives, capers, garlic, mint and lemon juice, and process briefly. Add enough oil through the feeder tube to make a thick paste. Taste and add salt and pepper accordingly.

2 The tapenade should be stored in the fridge, covered, for a couple of weeks before using for the best flavour.

Seaweed 'Tartare Sauce'

In Orkney, there is an enterprising young man called Karl Adamson
who runs Orkney Fine Food. Brought up in Stromness, he was always
down on the shore 'on the ebb', as a child. Now he and his small team
of workers gather kelp by hand along the shore whenever the tides
are suitable in the Hoy Sound, which is far enough west of Scapa Flow
to ensure there is no contamination of the seaweed from the First
World War wrecks. He then washes it, cures it overnight then minces it.
Finally, it is mixed with mayonnaise and some lemon (or garlic or chilli)
to make the most delicious tartare-sauce-like seaweed dip that is far
more exquisite than the original. Even before Karl mixes the cured
kelp with the mayonnaise the taste is good: it is just like capers
with a sea tang.

To pickle kelp, soak dried kelp (or thoroughly wash fresh) for a
good half hour. Meanwhile, place about double the amount of vinegar
to water (about 200ml/7 fl oz/^{1}/$_3$ pint vinegar to 100ml/3^1/$_2$ fl oz water) in
a large pan with a few peppercorns and bay leaves. Add 4 tablespoons
sugar and bring slowly to the boil then, once the sugar is dissolved,
add the kelp and simmer for about 4–5 minutes, then remove and
strain off the kelp. Finely chop or mince this then proceed as below.

SERVES 6–8
2 tablespoons cured/pickled minced kelp
4 tablespoons fresh mayonnaise
salt and freshly ground black pepper

1 Mix the kelp and mayonnaise
together and season to taste.

2 Serve with a seafood platter
(or with chip-shop fish and chips).

Dulse and Oatmeal Soup
with Hot-smoked Trout

This recipe can be made every day, not just after a day's beachcombing, as it uses dried dulse.

If you cannot find hot-smoked trout, try hot-smoked salmon or even smoked mackerel as they are also good with this gutsy and utterly delicious soup.

SERVES 4

40g/1¹/₂ oz dried dulse, washed then soaked in warm water
    for 10 minutes and drained
2 large potatoes, peeled and diced
1 large leek, trimmed and chopped
25g/1 oz medium oatmeal
10g/¹/₄ oz fresh parsley
salt and freshly ground black pepper
2 fillets of hot-smoked trout and extra virgin olive oil, to serve

1 Place the drained dulse in a pan with the potatoes, leek and about 750ml/ 25 fl oz cold water. Season, bring to the boil then cover and simmer for about 10 minutes.

2 Mix the oatmeal in a cup with about 3 tablespoons of the cooking liquor then gradually add this into the soup, stirring well. (Don't worry if lumps form as it is all about to be blitzed.) Cook gently for 5 minutes then tip everything into a food processor or blender with the parsley, and process (you will have to do this in batches).

3 Check the seasoning and return to the pan. Reheat and serve in warm bowls. Flake the trout and place on top of the soup then drizzle over some oil just before serving.

Pickled Herring in Seaweed

Rolling herring into rollmops is always a slippery business, although the end result is good. Here I have rolled the fish first in dried seaweed (having tried several, I find nori is best); this not only adds an extra layer of colour but also makes the rolling procedure a good deal easier.

Nori is of course most commonly used for sushi; it can also be toasted and crumbled over salads or vegetables.

SERVES 3–4

6–8 herring fillets, skinned (each about 40–50g/1^1/$_2$–1^3/$_4$ oz)
3–4 teaspoons horseradish relish (or wasabi paste)
2 sheets nori (edible seaweed)
1 medium onion, peeled and finely sliced
3 or 4 bay leaves
4 cloves
1 pinch of mace
1 heaped tablespoon black peppercorns
^{1}/$_2$ teaspoon allspice
125ml/4 fl oz white wine vinegar
125ml/4 fl oz distilled vinegar
125ml/4 fl oz water
1 heaped teaspoon soft brown sugar
salt and freshly ground black pepper

1 Sprinkle the flesh of the herring fillets with salt and pepper, then spread ^{1}/$_2$ teaspoon of the horseradish relish over each. Cut the nori sheets to the same width and length as the fillets, then lay the fish on to the nori and roll up tightly.

2 Place half the onion slices into an ovenproof dish with the bay leaves, then lay the fish on top, packing them tightly together, so they do not unroll. Top with the remaining onion.

3 In a saucepan, mix the cloves, mace, peppercorns, allspice, vinegars, water and sugar together, and bring to the boil. Simmer, covered, for 10 minutes, then allow to cool for 20–30 minutes. Meanwhile, preheat the oven to 180°C/350°F/Gas 4.

4 Pour the mixture from the saucepan over the herring, cover and place in the oven for 20–25 minutes. Remove and leave to cool in the liquid for several hours (or overnight). Refrigerate once cold and eat with brown or rye bread and butter.

Fresh Carragheen Pudding

Flavourings such as citrus zest or juice (Seville oranges are particularly good) and sugar can be added to this pudding according to taste. Margaret Horn from Auchmithie serves it with stewed rhubarb.

SERVES 6

55g/2 oz freshly picked carragheen, well washed
1 litre/1³/₄ pints full-fat milk
sugar and other flavourings, such as lemon or orange juice (optional)

1 Put the carragheen and milk into a pan and bring to the boil slowly, then simmer for about 30 minutes, or until the seaweed has become rather gelatinous. Add any flavourings now – sugar to taste and some lemon or orange juice. Strain into a bowl and leave to set somewhere cold.

2 Eat on its own or with stewed rhubarb or apples.

Rose Water Carragheen Pudding

There is a lovely recipe in an old *Scottish Women's Rural Institute Cookbook* for a carragheen pudding for invalids with no flavourings apart from a little sugar and an awful lot of sherry: perhaps it was no bad thing in the old days to take to one's bed while ill!

SERVES 6

a scant 20g/³/₄ oz dried carragheen, washed then soaked in warm water
    for 10 minutes and drained
500ml/18 fl oz full-fat milk
about 1 tablespoon sugar
2 tablespoons rose water

1 Place the drained carragheen in a pan with the milk and bring slowly to the boil. Simmer for about 10 minutes, stirring often, until the milk has thickened and the liquid is looking rather gelatinous.

2 Add 1 tablespoon sugar and the rose water, stir well then tip over a fine strainer into a glass bowl. Taste and add more sugar, if you like. Leave to set somewhere cold.

Cheese

In 1983 when the Reades moved to the island of Mull from Somerset to farm dairy cows, they could hardly have envisaged that the small cheeses they began to make in a bucket would end up being sold in huge 22kg truckles and be so much in demand that they can barely keep up.

But husband and wife team Chris and Jeff Reade manage admirably to maintain high standards with their award-winning Isle of Mull cheese. And, although they knew about milk and dairy farming, they had to learn cheese-making from scratch in the 200-year-old dairy that came with Sgriob-ruadh Farm, near Tobermory. Their cheese is made to a traditional Cheddar recipe and so is defined as 'Cheddar-style' but differs as, according to Chris, 'it is a product of here'. The water and soil are different, as are the herbs and draff (a by-product of ground-up malted barley from Tobermory's distillery) the cows eat – all giving the cheese a unique character.

The milk from their Friesian-cross Brown Swiss cows is all unpasteurised and is made into a cheese that is matured for at least 10 months in their cellars. The Reades would love to keep the cheese longer and mature it for more than a year, but in Chris's words, 'We just don't manage to keep it longer; we have so many orders'! Not only do they make the huge cloth-bound truckles, but also baby truckles, 700g in weight, which are in particular demand over the Christmas period. Although a Cheddar by definition, theirs is paler in colour and softer in texture and with a sharper flavour than those traditionally made in south-west England. Chris describes the taste as tangy, spicy and creamy. It is also wonderfully smooth and infinitely moreish, excellent eaten 'neat' with bread or biscuits or, in true Scottish New Year tradition, served with shortbread. The Reades also use it to bake cheesy oatcakes, cheese and onion tart and in all sorts of sauces and potato gratins.

They also now produce ewes' milk cheese from their own flock of Friesian sheep. Mornish, named after a Mull peninsula, is a mould-ripened Brie-style cheese; Iona Cromak (named after the island off the western tip of Mull) is a semi-soft cheese whose rind is washed in Iona whisky from the Tobermory distillery. Killiechronan (the name of the peninsula where they also farm) is a basket-moulded cheese in the style of, according to Chris, a 'shepherd's hut recipe' – in other words, rustic and simple.

All are delicious. And Mull is possibly the only Scottish island able to offer a cheeseboard with such a variety of different traditionally made farmhouse cheeses (hard and soft; cow and sheep), but all made on the one farm and by the same family.

And this family all – literally – muck in. Chris makes the cheeses with son Brendan. Jeff and son Garth look after the cows and sheep. Son Joe runs the now famous Island Organics Bakery, making excellent organic biscuits and also good bread and cakes in their Tobermory bakery. They started baking bread in 1994 to sell in the van which his parents drove all over Mull (a 120-mile round trip), to sell their milk in their pre-cheese-making days, and that worked well for a while. But when the ferries from Mull to Coll and Tiree (where they supplied bread daily) stopped, it was no longer financially viable, which is when they began baking their specialist organic biscuits that are now sought after nationwide. And, fortunately, one of the places they are for sale is the CalMac ferry. So, on my journey back to Oban and then home, I was able to enjoy one of Joe's Oat Crumbles with my latte.

Squash with Melted Cheese and Dunkers

This wonderfully rich dish is good made either with butternut squash or turnip (swede) but the latter will take much longer to cook. So start well in advance.

Serve with dunkers of either crudités (raw batons of carrot, celery or fennel) or with toast soldiers or grissini.

SERVES 2

1 butternut squash or turnip (swede), about 800g/1 lb 12 oz
extra virgin olive oil
1 tablespoon cornflour
3 tablespoons dry white wine
100g/3^1/$_2$ oz Loch Arthur or Isle of Mull Cheddar, grated
50ml/2 fl oz crème fraîche
1 heaped teaspoon Dijon mustard
salt and freshly ground black pepper

1 Preheat the oven to 200°C/400°F/ Gas 6. If using squash, cut in half lengthwise and scoop out all the seeds and fibres. If using turnip, trim the ends and cut in half. Set the squash or turnip in a tight-fitting oven dish. Drizzle with olive oil and cook in the oven for about 45–50 minutes for the squash or 1^1/$_2$–2 hours for the turnip, until the flesh is tender to the tip of a knife. Do not proceed until tender enough to eat.

2 Mix the cornflour and wine in a bowl and then stir in the cheese, crème fraîche and mustard. Season well.

3 For the turnip, scoop out the centre part, leaving a good thick wall and base. Leave the squash as is, as there is already a natural pocket for the cheese mixture. Spoon the cheese mixture into the squash or turnip and return to the oven. Cook for 30 minutes, or until golden and bubbling. Serve with dippers and dunkers.

Gooey Cheese Potatoes with Bacon

On Good Friday, 13 April 2001, 350 animals were killed in the foot-and-mouth cull at Loch Arthur Community in Dumfriesshire. Determined to remember that tragic day in a more uplifting way, the members of Loch Arthur Creamery made a batch of their unpasteurised organic Cheddar-style cheese with the last milking from the doomed dairy herd. The cheeses were stored away – and regularly tested – during the eight long weeks that cheese production ceased. Then, in late September 2001, that Good Friday cheese was entered in the prestigious British Cheese Awards and, for the first time ever, won a Gold Medal; it was truly outstanding.

The story of Loch Arthur is not all about serendipity, however. It is also about hard work, dedication and vision. The Loch Arthur Community is well known locally, as it produces organic vegetables and fruit for the farm shop, raises organic beef and dairy cattle and sheep, bakes bread in their own bakery and of course makes world-class cheese. But it is also unique in Scotland, as the community of some 75 people includes 30 adults with learning difficulties, all of whom share in the work. A visit to Loch Arthur is humbling not only to see the fruits of the labours of so many devoted people but also to taste and see that the most natural ingredients do indeed make the best food.

It all began through necessity: they needed to use up excess milk from their dairy herd. In the small, modern creamery, I saw the delicious semi-soft Criffel used in this recipe being made and the Loch Arthur Farmhouse cheeses in the presses, ready to be turned, scalded and wrapped in delicate mantles of muslin. After some 6 months' maturing, during which time they are carefully turned and wiped, they are ready to be sold.

SERVES 2-3

500g/1 lb 2 oz new potatoes, scrubbed
1 large onion, peeled and chopped (not finely)
2 tablespoons extra virgin olive oil
100g/3^1/$_2$ oz dry-cure bacon, chopped
150g/5^1/$_2$ oz semi-soft farmhouse cheese such as Criffel (or Carola from Moray)
salt and freshly ground black pepper

1 Boil the potatoes until just tender then drain well and cut into large chunks.

2 Fry the onion in the oil for 10 minutes, or until golden, then add the bacon and fry until done.

3 Tip everything into a small gratin dish.

4 Remove and discard the rind from the cheese, chop the cheese then scatter it over the potatoes. Season well.

5 Bake at 200°C/400°F/Gas 6 for 15–20 minutes, or until the cheese is molten and gooey. Eat hot with bread and salad.

Isle of Mull Cheese Oatcakes

Cheese was described as 'milk's leap toward immortality' by Clifton Fadiman, the US editor, in 1957. And whether you eat it just as it is or converted into divine oatcakes such as these, a good cheese is always memorable.

My recipe is based on Shelagh Reade's; Shelagh, married to Brendan Reade, makes her cheesy oatcakes for the farm shop on Mull during the busy summer months. Do not even think about adding salt or other flavouring, as farmhouse cheese has enough taste all by itself. When not serving with the very obvious cheese and pickle – or soup or salad – I also like to serve them with slivers of Mull Cheddar and thin slices of quince paste (membrillo).

MAKES 12
100g/3¹/₂ oz porridge oats
100g/3¹/₂ oz medium oatmeal
125g/4¹/₂ oz Isle of Mull (or other farmhouse) Cheddar, finely grated
75g/2³/₄ oz butter, melted

1 Preheat the oven to 170°C/325°F/Gas 3. Mix the oats, oatmeal and cheese in a large bowl then slowly drizzle in the melted butter. Stir briefly with a wooden spoon to combine, adding just enough boiling water to form a firm paste, about 1¹/₂ tablespoons.

2 Using hands dipped in flour (or if you want them to be 100 per cent wheat-free, dip in fine oatmeal) bring the dough together in your hands then pat out on a board. Just use the heels of your hands, not a rolling pin. Once it is reasonably thin, cut out 12 rounds. Place on a lightly buttered baking sheet and bake in the oven for 30–35 minutes, or until they have crisped up and are golden brown. Cool on a wire rack.

Criffel and Courgette Pizza

A great favourite from Loch Arthur Creamery, Criffel is a semi-soft, organic, rind-washed cheese with a smooth, deep flavour – ideal for cooking, as it melts into a soft delicate goo and so is perfect for dishes such as this one. If you cannot find it, or another British semi-soft cheese with a medium-strong, but not mild, flavour, then brie will do.

SERVES 2
400g/14 oz strong white flour
1¹/₂ teaspoons salt
7g sachet of fast-action/easy-blend dried yeast
1 tablespoon extra virgin olive oil
FOR THE TOPPING
6 tablespoons passata
1 large courgette, thinly sliced
200g/7 oz Criffel, rind removed, thinly sliced
10–12 anchovies
extra virgin olive oil, to drizzle

1 Place the flour in a bowl with the salt. Stir in the yeast then make a well in the centre.

2 Add the olive oil and about 250ml/9 fl oz tepid water – enough to make a softish dough. Turn on to a floured board and knead gently until smooth, about 8–10 minutes.

3 Place in a bowl, cover and leave somewhere warm for an hour or so until risen. Meanwhile, preheat the oven to 230°C/450°F/Gas 8. Punch down the dough and roll, or push out, to fit a large pizza plate or baking sheet (about 30cm/12 in).

4 Smear over the passata, then top with the courgette slices and then the cheese and anchovies. Finally, trickle a tiny amount of oil around the crust, to give it a good sheen. Bake for 15–20 minutes, or until cooked through. Serve hot with salad.

Chocolate and Grimbister Cheese Tart

This exquisite recipe is based on one I enjoyed at the Kirkwall Hotel
and was the idea of Chef Bruce Mainland from the Orkney island of
Rousay. His recipe was for chopped chocolate and Grimbister cheese
set in an egg custard tart. Mine has a base of gooey molten chocolate
and a creamy chocolate-flecked topping that has the merest hint of
cheese. Grimbister is a traditional farmhouse cheese made on the
mainland of Orkney. It is fresh and crumbly with a nice fruity
aftertaste and is not dissimilar to Wensleydale. Indeed, if you
cannot find Grimbister cheese use this instead.

SERVES 6–8

150g/5¹/₂ oz plain flour, sifted
50g/1³/₄ oz ground almonds
25g/1 oz golden caster sugar
85g/3 oz butter, diced
1 large free-range egg

FOR THE FILLING

200g/7 oz dark chocolate (minimum 70 per cent cocoa solids), coarsely grated
125g/4¹/₂ oz Grimbister cheese, grated
1 large free-range egg and 2 large egg yolks
100ml/3¹/₂ fl oz double cream
100ml/3¹/₂ fl oz milk
85g/3 oz golden caster sugar
cocoa powder, to dust

1 To make the pastry, place the
flour, almonds and sugar in a food
processor, blend then add the butter
and process briefly until it resembles
breadcrumbs. Add the beaten egg
slowly through the feeder tube.
Alternatively, rub the butter into
the flour mixture by hand and stir
in the egg.

2 Bring the dough together in your
hands, wrap in clingfilm and chill
for an hour or so.

3 Roll out the pastry to fit a shallow
23cm/9 in tart tin and prick all over.
Refrigerate for at least 2 hours (or
freeze for 30 minutes). Meanwhile,
preheat the oven to 200°C/400°F/
Gas 6.

4 Line the pastry case with foil, fill
with baking beans, and bake blind
for 15 minutes. Remove the foil and
beans, and continue to bake for 5
minutes before removing from the
oven. While the pastry is hot, scatter

over the grated chocolate. Leave to cool slightly (10 minutes is fine) then set on a baking sheet. Reduce the oven temperature to 180°C/350°F/Gas 4.

5 Place the cheese, eggs, cream, milk and sugar in a food processor and whiz until blended, then slowly pour this into the pastry case. It will be very full so walk carefully with it to the oven. Bake for about 30 minutes, or until just set in the middle; there will still be a tiny wobble if shaken lightly.

6 Leave for at least 30 minutes then dust with cocoa and serve barely warm.

Picnic with cousins Lynda and Ross, Edinburgh, 1959

Oats

'A grain, which in England is generally given to horses, but in Scotland supports the people' was how Dr Samuel Johnson, the eighteenth-century essayist and lexicographer, defined oats in his famous dictionary. This was a dig at the prevailing Scottish poverty, but it also accurately described the virtual monopoly oats have had in the Scottish diet for centuries. As a Scot, I was brought up on oats. There were oatcakes, flapjacks, bannocks and, of course, porridge. Soups were thickened with oatmeal; apple crumbles topped with oat flakes; skirlie, made from toasted oats and onion, used to stuff chicken or to serve with mince. With the increasing awareness nowadays of the valuable contribution oats play in a healthy diet – this low-GI (glycaemic index) cereal is high in zinc, protein, iron, B vitamins, calcium and cholesterol-reducing soluble fibre – we all ought to be making more of an effort to include oats in our everyday diets, so why not begin each day with porridge? Porridge has been described as the new sushi, with oats sales growing year on year. In the US, there is a new chain called Cereality specialising in porridge (which the Americans call 'oatmeal') with various toppings as diverse as coconut and peanut butter. In Scotland, there is now a peripatetic 'porridge bar' going round fairs and shows serving bowls of the hot stuff – and the long queues are testament to its popularity. Scottish farmer David Henderson, who died in 1998 aged 109, swore by a diet of porridge, prunes and an improbable mixture of gin and cattle salts. I like to think it was the porridge that encouraged longevity and not the gin – or even the cattle salts!

In rural areas, there was also the 'porridge drawer', a prime example of Scottish thrift. Vast pots of porridge would be cooked, then poured directly into the drawer in the kitchen dresser (called a 'kist' in the north-east of Scotland). It was allowed to cool and become solid, then cut into sections and taken on to the hills, as sustenance for the hard day's work. (In the evening, slices called 'calders' were cut off and fried then served with eggs or fish, not unlike grilled or fried polenta.) Bill McConachie, one of the engineers at Grampian Oats recalls the cold porridge in the drawer in his kitchen being cut and eaten for anything from one week to ten days! Hebridean fisherman and guga-hunter, Dods Macfarlane, remembers older folk in the north of Lewis telling him of a similar tradition, originating in dire necessity, since, apart from porridge, there was very little else to eat and so the morning's pan would be made to last longer than breakfast.

During a visit to Grampian Oat Products at their large factory near Banff, Aberdeenshire, I witnessed the modern processing of oats. Having been sown in March or April, they are usually ready for cutting around the middle to the end of August. Oats come from farms from the Black Isle, Morayshire and Aberdeenshire in the north and as far south as Perthshire and northern Fife. The advantage of such a wide distribution of farmers means that if rain is hindering the progress of the cereal in Inverness, there is a good chance that the crop further south in Perth is faring better.

The two main varieties of oats, Matra and Dula are described as 'reliable old favourites'. It is these two varieties that account for about two-thirds of the company's oats; others are chosen according to compatibility with the soil and climatic conditions of each contracted farm. The climate of Scotland suits oats perfectly. Because of the average annual temperature, growth is slow and there is little danger of the crop ripening too quickly under a sweltering summer sun. Cool temperatures mean the kernels develop and fill out very gradually, and so they become plump and full of flavour.

Once they are accepted as suitable, the raw oats are graded, cleaned and then dried in silos, before being removed, according to demand, then milled. The hulling process, by a machine called a 'paddy separator', removes the outer husks from the oats, to leave only the kernel. A total of 13 further processing operations are then carried out, to ensure the oat kernels, or 'groats', do not contain any loose husk fibres or other impurities.

As well as visiting a large oat producer, I was also fortunate to see a small-scale producer milling oats in the old-fashioned way. It took place at Montgarrie Mills near Alford, Aberdeenshire on a crisp, cold spring day. High above the roaring coal fire and under the huge domed chimney, I was able to stand on a bed of hot toasty oats (still in their husks so no worries on the hygiene front) and help turn them with a long-handled sheeler (wooden shovel) as they slowly dried over the heat of the coal fire three floors below. Not only was the warmth and feel of those grains underfoot unforgettable but also the smell of toasty nutty oats was sublime. It was a comforting bowl of porridge on a tropical beach.

A reality check brought me back to my surroundings when Donald Macdonald, who is production manager in the mill his great-grandfather bought in 1894, lead me off the heated, oaty carpet. The cleaned, locally grown oats had been laid out on the traditional flat kiln floor to dry for about four hours, turned to ensure even drying, until they have a moisture content of only 4.5 per cent – far lower than most producers. This might take longer but the resulting flavour is intensely oaty and nutty. Once they have cooled down (which can take up to ten days) the oats are screened then put through two shelling stones, one to open the longest grains, the second to open the shorter husks. They are then ground into the four cuts (fine, medium, rough and pinhead) and finally packed.

The oatmeal from Alford has the most fabulous rich taste and wonderful texture, perhaps because of its low moisture content or perhaps because it is processed in the time-honoured way. The mill is still powered by a massive water wheel (some 7.5 metres in diameter) built in 1882. And as I was standing outside (now with cold, decidedly unhappy feet) watching 'her' (Donald refers to the wheel as 'she') slowly crank into action as the sluice gates let in water from the Essett burn, there was a Heath Robinson moment, for inside the mill, the shelling stones began to turn, the riddles (large-meshed sieves) rhythmically shook and the millstones ground round and round.

In these days of high-speed, high-tech food manufacturing, seeing a mill such as Alford in full production creates an overwhelming sense of history. It also bestows a sense of pride that Scotland is still producing such quality raw ingredients, ready to be converted into traditional and modern dishes.

Proper Porridge

'The grey, bubbling mass in the black pot' is how author G.W. Lockhart described the morning porridge he hated. I saw it more as manna from heaven and ate my daily bowl with relish. And although as a child my morning porridge was allowed to be 'besmirched' with brown sugar and top of the milk, just one generation back, this was unheard of, as my parents ate it in the traditional way: hot porridge was ladled into bowls (usually wooden) and a smaller bowl containing milk placed alongside. Then, with your spoon (usually horn), you took a spoonful of porridge, dipped it into the milk bowl then ate it. This meant the porridge stayed hot and the milk cold longer. It was embellished only with salt, never sugar. Porridge was, interestingly, always referred to as 'they' – and 'they' were traditionally eaten standing up, never seated.

As judge of the 12th Annual World Porridge-making Championships in Carrbridge in the Highlands, I was amazed at how different 35 bowls of porridge could taste; yes, that is the number we judges waded through. After the difference in texture, which depends on the grade of oatmeal used (only oatmeal is allowed, not porridge oats), the most crucial factor in the taste was salt. Oversalt and it is inedible; undersalt and it is tasteless. Everyone cooked with water, not milk. One contestant roasted his oatmeal first, which gave the most splendidly nutty flavour. 'Grey, bubbling mass' I most certainly did not see; rather, 35 different ways to interpret a versatile dish made from only three ingredients: oatmeal, water and salt. Nothing simpler – although after 35 bowls, I admit I saw porridge in a slightly less enthusiastic way than I do every winter morning at home.

F. Marian McNeill's recipe for porridge is one that many people still use. Instead of soaking the oatmeal overnight then cooking the next day, it was slowly released through the fingers of a clenched fist while stirring madly with the spurtle – the long wooden stick used specifically for porridge (one of my grandfathers called it a 'theevil' and this name is also still used). I was brought up with the soaking overnight method and it is still my preferred one. If, however, you have forgotten to soak oatmeal and you wake up to a blizzard outside, then you can still make proper porridge with oatmeal: you will just need a little longer to cook it.

If, however, you are using rolled or porridge oats (which have less flavour than oatmeal, as they are already steamed or part-cooked), you will need a cup of oats to about $2^{1}/_{4}$ cups of water and reduce the cooking time to 3–4 minutes. Medium oatmeal is the most commonly used, but coarse oatmeal makes good porridge. But my favourite, for its rough, nubbly texture and full flavour, is pinhead. And with the various cuts or grades of oatmeal, every single day of the week can be different, whether you use half medium oatmeal, half porridge oats or half pinhead, half coarse oatmeal – both texture and flavour varies from day to day.

Or you can do a modern-day version of the porridge drawer, using your freezer: make a batch of proper oatmeal porridge (preferably with pinhead) and freeze in seven freezer bags, then, each morning, plop the contents into a pan with a splash of milk and heat gently until piping hot.

SERVES 3–4
1 cup of medium, coarse or pinhead oatmeal
about 3 cups of cold water
salt

1 Ideally, soak the oatmeal overnight in the water. (Or simply start from scratch in a pan in the morning.)

2 Next day, bring slowly to the boil then add a good pinch of salt. Stirring frequently (preferably with a spurtle), cook for 3–4 minutes if pre-soaked; about 5 minutes if not (allowing 10–15 minutes if using all pinhead) over a medium to low heat, until thick and creamy. Add some boiling water if the porridge is too thick.

3 Serve at once in warm bowls with a moat of cold milk. (I also like either a sprinkling of wheatgerm or a few flakes of sea salt; I have eschewed my childhood sugar days.)

Chocolate Cranachan with Raspberries

Cranachan is delicious, but traditionally only eaten at harvest time with seasonal fruit such as brambles, so I decided to make a variation using dark chocolate and hazelnuts. The result is a rich, luscious dessert of contrasting layers of cream, chocolate, raspberries, nuts and toasted oats. It looks best served in a large glass bowl, to show the different layers to their best advantage. Start this the day before you intend serving it, so all the flavours combine well.

SERVES 8–10

200g/7 oz whole rolled oats
150g/5¹/₂ oz toasted hazelnuts, chopped
about 100g/3¹/₂ oz light muscovado sugar
175g/6 oz quality dark chocolate, grated
85g/3 oz quality milk chocolate, grated
600ml/20 fl oz/1 pint double cream
150ml/5 fl oz/¹/₄ pint Drambuie or Loch Fyne Liqueur
500ml/18 fl oz crème fraîche
450g/1 lb raspberries

1 Toast the oats by spreading them on to a foil-lined baking tray and placing this under a preheated grill, for 3–4 minutes, or until the oats are golden brown. Stir them every 30 seconds or so, to ensure they do not burn.

2 Mix together the hazelnuts and sugar, add the grated chocolate then tip in the very hot oats, directly from the grill. Stir everything together well until the chocolate melts. Allow to cool then break up a little as it tends to form clumps. In another bowl, whip the double cream until it is thick, but still slightly floppy. Gently fold in the Drambuie or liqueur and crème fraîche. Divide the raspberries into three.

3 In a large glass dish, spoon in a third of the oat mixture, then layer a third of the Drambuie cream. Lightly crush a third of the raspberries and sprinkle on top. (Sprinkle over 1–2 teaspoons of sugar if the berries are very tart.) Spoon over another third of the oats then another third of cream. Crush another third of the raspberries (with more sugar if necessary), sprinkle on top then scatter over the last oats and a final layer of cream. Smooth over the surface, cover and refrigerate for at least 24 hours.

4 Next day, decorate with the remaining third of whole raspberries.

Oatmeal Pancakes From 1755

Oh, they knew a thing or two about cooking in the 1700s. I took a recipe from Elizabeth Cleland's *New and Easy Method of Cookery* (1755) for oatmeal pancakes and just slung all the raw ingredients together, expecting it to form a thick smooth batter, like a regular pancake batter. Had I read more carefully, however, the author stipulates boiling the milk first then adding the oatmeal so that it is almost porridge-like and therefore thick enough to convert into pancakes. The original recipe called for 'a chopin of milk' to be boiled and a 'mutchkin of oatmeal' to be stirred in first. The flavourings below (lemon and nutmeg) are precisely what Mrs Cleland wrote. And her serving suggestion was: 'serve hot with beaten butter, orange and sugar'; I recommend serving warm with *Raspberry Curd* (see page 183), jam, or with *Fairy Butter* (see page 215).

They are delightfully light yet with a good and interesting texture from the oatmeal.

MAKES 12–14
300ml/10 fl oz/^{1}/$_2$ pint milk
125g/4^1/$_2$ oz medium oatmeal
1 large free-range egg, beaten
25g/1 oz golden caster sugar
grating of nutmeg
grated zest of 1 small unwaxed lemon
^{1}/$_4$ teaspoon baking powder
a pinch of salt
butter, for greasing

1 Bring the milk to the boil then remove from the heat and gradually stir in the oatmeal. At this stage, I like to get in with a balloon whisk and whisk well to ensure there are no lumps. Allow to cool then beat in the remaining ingredients.

2 Heat a girdle (griddle; or heavy frying pan) to medium-hot and lightly wipe with butter. Once hot, drop spoonfuls of the batter on to the surface and cook as for Scotch pancakes: 2–3 minutes one side then, once large bubbles appear, flip over and continue to cook the other side. After 1–2 minutes remove and keep warm.

Oatcake Tartlets with Cauli Purée and Salmon Roe

These make delicious canapés with a glass of champagne.

MAKES 24

200g/7 oz cauliflower (1 small or 2 baby caulis), in florets
about 100ml/3¹/₂ fl oz single cream
15g/¹/₂ oz butter
24 oatcake tartlet cases (or mini-oatcakes)
100g/3¹/₂ oz jar of salmon roe (keta)
salt and freshly ground black pepper

1 Cook the cauliflower in boiling salted water until just tender, then drain well. Whiz in a blender with the cream and the butter, plenty of black pepper and salt to taste. (You might need more cream; the correct consistency is a soft, not-too-sloppy purée.)

2 While still warm, use to fill the cases then top with a heaped teaspoonful of salmon roe. Serve at once.

Salmon with a Herby Oatmeal Crust

Serve with couscous and salad.

SERVES 3

3 salmon fillets, skinned, pin bones removed
2 tablespoons extra virgin olive oil, plus extra for brushing
75g/2³/₄ oz oatmeal (half pinhead, half medium)
the zest of 1 small unwaxed lemon
3 tablespoons fresh chopped herbs, such as parsley, mint and chervil
salt and freshly ground black pepper

1 Preheat the oven to 220°C/425°F/ Gas 7 and oil a baking sheet. Brush the salmon all over with oil.

2 Combine the oatmeal, lemon zest and herbs, and season with salt and pepper. Place on a plate. Dip the rounded surface of each fillet into the mixture, then place on the baking sheet. Cook on the top shelf of the oven for about 10 minutes, or until just done. Test by inserting the tip of a sharp knife into the centre; the flesh should flake easily and be cooked through.

Porridge Scones with Cream and Brown Sugar

The origin of this bizarre-sounding recipe is a Second World War recipe booklet, with a foreword by Lord Woolton (appointed Minister of Food in 1940). Their version was made with cold porridge instead of milk or egg to bind – thrift in a porridge bowl! I have adapted the recipe by adding a little cream and brown sugar.

It goes without saying that the better your porridge, the better your scone; I like a combination of oat flakes and pinhead oatmeal. Eat the scones warm with thick cream (preferably clotted) and raspberry jam.

MAKES 8

50g/1³/₄ oz medium oatmeal
150g/5¹/₂ oz self-raising flour, sifted
25g/1 oz light muscovado sugar
1 teaspoon baking powder
a pinch of salt
250g/9 oz cold (unrefrigerated) cooked porridge, about 1 small bowl
75–100 ml/2¹/₂–3¹/₂ fl oz double cream (preferably almost 'off')

1 Preheat the oven to 230°C/450°F/ Gas 8 and lightly oil a baking sheet. Combine the oatmeal, flour, sugar and baking powder in a bowl with the salt. Gently work in the porridge with your hands then add just enough cream so that the dough will come together loosely in your hands.

2 Pat out on a board to about 2.5cm/1 in thick and cut into eight. Transfer to the prepared baking sheet. (Alternatively, shape into two rounds, transfer to the baking sheet and slash lightly into four.) Place near the top of the oven for 15–20 minutes (20 minutes for the two rounds) then transfer carefully to a wire rack.

Warm Raspberry Porridge

As well as the regular porridge category at the World Porridge-making Championships, there is a speciality section and my year of judging found us supping porridge with smoked salmon (tasty, if a little salty), cloudberries (from an eager Swedish contestant), marshmallows and melted tablet (divine) and seaweed (interesting!). Lynn Benge's warm porridge with raspberries was a favourite – rather like a warm cranachan. This is my adaptation of her recipe.

50g/1³/₄ oz medium oatmeal
about 25g/1 oz light muscovado sugar
75 ml/2¹/₂ fl oz Columba Cream liqueur, or other whisky-based cream liqueur
175g/6 oz raspberries, puréed or blended
150ml/5 fl oz/¹/₄ pint double cream, lightly whipped
fresh raspberries, to decorate

1 Place the oatmeal, 300ml/10 fl oz/ ¹/₂ pint cold water and the sugar in a pan and bring slowly to the boil, stirring well. Once boiling, reduce the heat and simmer, stirring, for 5 minutes, or until thick. Remove from the heat and stir in the whisky liqueur.

2 Set aside for 10 minutes, stirring occasionally, then stir in the raspberries. Finally, fold in the cream and taste (some berries are more tart than others; if still rather too sharp, stir in a little extra sugar). Serve at once, decorated with fresh berries.

Gooseberry Crisp
Eat warm with thick cream.

SERVES 4
400g/14 oz gooseberries
125g/4¹/₂ oz golden caster sugar
1 tablespoon elderflower cordial
75g/2³/₄ oz plain flour, sifted
75g/2³/₄ oz whole rolled oats
100g/3¹/₂ oz butter, diced

1 Preheat the oven to 190°C/375°F/ Gas 5. Place the gooseberries in a small oven dish and sprinkle over 25g/1 oz sugar. Drizzle over the cordial.

2 Place the flour, oats and the remaining sugar in a bowl then rub in the butter. Tip over the berries and pack down lightly. Bake for 35–40 minutes, or until bubbling and golden.

Barley

I can think of few places in the world where there is such evidence of the similarity of diet spanning 5,000 years. But in Orkney, the flourishing archipelago of 70 islands, I was lucky enough to visit the fascinating Skara Brae, a Neolithic village dating back to 3,100BC (centuries before the Pyramids of Giza were built), and a short 7-mile hike up the coast to the Barony Mills at Birsay.

At Skara Brae, you can see the actual houses from the Middle Stone Age with the central fire and a large stone (to cook their bread or bannocks on) at the side. You can see the 'saddle querns' where barley was ground between two stones. And it is known that as well as sea birds such as fulmars, gannet and auks, those early people ate shellfish, fish, cheese, meat, game – and barley. This diet pretty much reflects the diet nowadays, apart from the sea birds, but the interesting feature to me is barley. It would have been the ancient variety of barley known as bere. Nowadays, although it has become rather rare following the commonplace switch to the more commercial types of barley, bere growing and milling are still very much alive and well on Orkney.

The saddle querns of Neolithic times gave way to trough querns in the Bronze Age then rotary querns in the Iron Age, and finally the more sophisticated water-powered wheel, introduced by the Norseman, to grind the grain. By the end of the seventeenth century there were at least 50 mills in Orkney; nowadays there is just one working mill.

And so it was, one bitterly cold winter's day, that I stood inside the tall Victorian water mill at Barony Mills with the wind whipping outside against the weatherworn stone. Miller Ray Philips, whose father and grandfather had also been millers here, showed me what occupies his working day during the long winter months. (In the summer, the mill becomes a tourist attraction.)

The bere, formerly known by its Norse name of *bygg*, arrives at the mill and is dried down to a moisture level of about 8–10 per cent, ready for grinding. The great wheel outside the mill then creaks into action as the sluice gates open and the enormous weight of water causes the wheel to turn slowly. The dried grain is then taken to the stones, which remove the dust and the husks then mill it into flour. 'Grap' is the term for the unsieved, roughly ground bere that is always ground to a fine meal then sieved and bagged for customers. Ray laughed at first when I asked him if I could have some of the coarsely milled grap to make bere porridge. No one does this on Orkney; porridge is always made from oatmeal, he told me. But I thought of my time living in Finland where porridge is made from barley as well as oats and rice. I thought of polenta made usually from maize but sometimes in Italy's Alpine valleys from buckwheat, which has a not dissimilar earthy flavour. Ray insisted it tastes like wallpaper paste, but I was determined to give it a try. I should have realised at this stage that if an Orcadian told me how to do – or not do – something relating to barley, to listen.

So, Ray kindly sieved an entire batch of grap and, with a knowing smile, presented a bag to me for my porridge. Once home, I could hardly wait, and yet, even made with half bere, half oats, I have to admit, it was not nice. The texture was not too bad since it was coarsely ground. It was more the taste that was unpleasant: I thought it tasted beery; my husband thought it was reminiscent of cattle fodder. Ray, you were right and I was wrong. (Although, how you know what wallpaper paste tastes like beats me.)

Cheat's Bere Blinis

Once you have tasted blinis (cheat's ones use a raising agent instead of yeast) made with beremeal instead of buckwheat flour you will never want to revert to the classic recipe again.

These are good served with a smear of sour cream, into which you have stirred some horseradish sauce, and then top with a twirl of smoked salmon or trout. A frond of dill will finish it off (or a spoonful of caviar if you are feeling Russian – or extravagant).

Make in regular blini size for a starter or little one-bite-size blinis for canapés.

Barley flour also works well here.

MAKES 12 BLINIS OR 24–30 COCKTAIL BITE-SIZE BLINIS

75g/2³/₄ oz self-raising flour, sifted
50g/1³/₄ oz beremeal
1 level teaspoon baking powder
1 large free-range egg
150ml/5 fl oz/¹/₄ pint milk
butter, for greasing
salt

1 Place the flour and beremeal, baking powder, egg, milk and a good pinch of salt in a food processor and process until smooth (or whisk by hand with a balloon whisk).

2 Place a large heavy-based frying pan or girdle (griddle) on a medium heat and lightly butter the surface, using kitchen paper. When the pan is sufficiently hot (test by dropping a teaspoon of batter on to the surface: it should bubble within 1 minute) drop 1 dessertspoon of batter into the pan and repeat three times to make four pancakes. After 1–2 minutes you will see bubbles, so that is the sign to flip over. Cook for a further 1 minute or so, until batter does not ooze out when lightly pressed with your fingers.

3 Remove to a wire rack and cover loosely with a tea towel. Continue making the pancakes until all the batter is used up.

Bere Bannocks

This is my adaptation of Paul Doull's recipe from Foveran Hotel near Kirkwall. Paul had forgotten I was coming for my bannock lesson early one chilly February morning but after 10 minutes' of phoning, I eventually got through to him; an impressive 3 minutes later he arrived, straight from the school run. Within a mere 15 minutes, there on the wire rack, covered with a tea towel to keep them moist, were the most beautiful bannocks, speckled all over with charred marks. And devouring them 10 minutes later with Orkney butter and coffee (the latter from another, perhaps warmer, island), I looked out from his dining room window to Scapa Flow and the islands beyond. It was impossible to feel anything other than thoroughly at one with the world.

MAKES 1 BANNOCK, TO BE DIVIDED INTO 4 PIECES

70g/2^1/$_2$ oz beremeal
70g/2^1/$_2$ oz self-raising flour
1 level teaspoon bicarbonate of soda
1 rounded teaspoon cream of tartar
^{1}/$_4$ teaspoon salt
^{1}/$_2$ tablespoon vegetable oil, plus extra for greasing

1 First put the girdle (griddle) or solid frying pan on the stove to heat to a steady heat. This can take a good 10 minutes. Very lightly oil the surface.

2 Mix the beremeal and flour, bicarbonate of soda, cream of tartar and salt in a large bowl. Make a well in the middle and add the oil then enough cold water to combine to a soft dough (I use 150ml/5 fl oz/^{1}/$_4$ pint).

3 Tip on to a board dusted with a little beremeal and shape gently into a bannock shape: a round about 15–17cm/ 6–6^1/$_2$ in diameter and about 2–2.5cm/ ^{3}/$_4$–1 in thick (it puffs up as it cooks). Use a very light touch and do not knead.

4 Slap it on to the girdle and cook, without poking or touching, for 5 minutes, and then turn and continue to cook for 4 minutes. Both top and bottom will be scorched all over with a golden brown. Remove and place on a wire rack, loosely cover with a tea towel to keep the top soft. Tempting though it is to devour hot, leave until cold before splitting open and spreading with a little butter. Classically served with oily fish such as herring or with Orkney cheese, they are also excellent with anchovies or fish pâté.

Barley Bread

Since there is no barley milled commercially in Scotland now (only bere), I like to use Dove Farm's barley flour for this, milled at their farm in Berkshire from barley grown for them within a 10-mile radius. The variety of barley they mill is called 'Cellar'.

This is a lovely loaf with an almost chewy texture and a terrific flavour that is deep without being too earthy. Rather like bannocks, this is good served with a ewe's or goat's milk cheese and oily fish such as herring. It makes excellent toast.

MAKES 2 LOAVES

200g/7 oz barley flour
450/1 lb unbleached strong white flour, sifted
40g/1½ oz barley flakes or sunflower seeds
7g sachet of fast-action/easy-blend dried yeast
2 teaspoons salt
2 tablespoons sunflower oil

1 Mix the flours, barley flakes or sunflower seeds and yeast in a bowl with the salt. Make a well in the centre, pour in the oil then slowly add enough tepid water (400–425ml/ 14–15 fl oz/³/₄ pint) to make a softish dough.

2 Using floured hands, bring the dough together and turn out on to a floured board. Sprinkling lightly with flour, if necessary, knead for 10 minutes, or until smooth; it should be soft and shiny-looking but not too sticky.

3 Place in an oiled bowl and cover with clingfilm, then leave somewhere warm for 2–2½ hours until well risen.

4 Punch down and divide into two, then shape into two round loaves about 18cm/7 in in diameter. Place on oiled baking sheets and cover with oiled clingfilm. Leave to rise again, somewhere warm, for about 1 hour, or until well risen. (When ready, the dough will not spring back when gently pressed with your finger.) Meanwhile, preheat the oven to 230°C/450°F/Gas 8.

5 Slash the tops of the loaves lightly with a knife to form slits then dust lightly with flour and bake in the oven for 25–30 minutes, or until the base sounds hollow when tapped.

Oven-cooked Barley with Mushrooms and Parsley

I hesitate to call this dish a risotto as the very notion of using barley instead of rice – and cooking it in the oven – is anathema to risotto purists. But the method is similar. I like this served with roast chicken or grilled salmon – or, as it is so delicious, just on its own.

Any leftovers can be made into the most delicious barley cake by puréeing 200g/7 oz of the mixture with about 50ml/2 fl oz water and adding 2 tablespoons freshly grated Parmesan cheese. Heat some olive oil to hot in a small frying pan and press in the barley mixture. Cook for 4–5 minutes, or until a crust forms, then carefully flip over and continue to cook until a crust forms underneath, about 3–4 minutes. Serve piping hot with maybe a fried egg on top.

SERVES 6

50g/1³/₄ oz butter
1 onion, peeled and chopped
2 celery sticks, chopped
2 fat garlic cloves, peeled and chopped
150g/5¹/₂ oz mushrooms, cut into chunks
300g/10¹/₂ oz pearl barley
450ml/16 fl oz hot chicken stock
1 tablespoon extra virgin olive oil
50g/1³/₄ oz freshly grated Parmesan cheese
20g/³/₄ oz flat-leaf parsley, chopped
salt and freshly ground black pepper

1 Preheat the oven to 170°C/325°F/ Gas 3. Heat the butter in a flameproof casserole dish and gently fry the onion, celery and garlic for 5 minutes, then stir in the mushrooms. Cook for 5 minutes then add the barley. Stir to coat in the butter then add the hot stock and ³/₄ teaspoon salt.

2 Grind in some black pepper and bring to the boil. Stir then cover and cook in the oven for 30–35 minutes, or until the liquid has all been absorbed. Stir in the oil, add the Parmesan, check the seasoning then stir in the parsley just before serving.

Barley Porridge

During the year I spent in the north of Finland I often had porridge for breakfast. There was, of course, oatmeal porridge but it was also made from rye flakes, rice and barley. Like Scottish porridge, this was a salty affair, seldom besmirched with sugar. Since it is made with milk there is no need to add it at the end as we would with our Scots porridge.

This recipe for barley porridge (*ohrauunipuuro*) is from my friend Ritva who lives in Kemi in the far north of Finland. She serves it with a runny jam or 'berry soup' made by cooking fresh blueberries, raspberries or lingonberries, sweetening to taste then thickening with potato flour. I like it with the merest trickle of runny honey.

SERVES 6
175g/6 oz pearl barley
700ml/1¼ pints milk
¾ teaspoon salt

1 Preheat the oven to 150°C/300°F/ Gas 2. Place the barley, milk and 500ml/18 fl oz water in an ovenproof dish, then stir in the salt.

2 Cover and cook in the oven for 3 hours, stirring after 1½ hours. Remove the lid at this time if you like a skin to form, rather like the one that forms on rice pudding.

Whisky Cake

I was delighted to visit a distillery to see whisky being made in the traditional manner on Speyside. Glenfiddich have been making whisky since 1887 and, although nowadays some barley must be imported to accommodate their requirements, local barley is used when possible. The barley is first steeped in water to start it germinating. Germination lasts about a week after which it is dried on a floor above the kiln. (The kiln is mostly coal-fired but some peat is added too; Islay whiskies use more peat smoke to give them their characteristic flavour.) This whole procedure is called 'malting' and it is the germination that converts the starch in the barley grain into sugar; the sugar is converted into alcohol later in the process once the yeast is added.

My recipe for whisky fruit cake was inspired by one made by Asher's the bakers in Nairn, a half-hour north of Speyside on the Moray Firth coast. The Asher family have been bakers since 1877, and, although they still produce the classic butteries, rolls, pies, excellent cakes, such as jap cakes, and all-butter puff-pastry apple turnovers, they diversified recently into the gift market, producing three varieties of whisky cake. One uses a whisky from the Islands, one from Speyside and one from the Highlands. The difference in flavour is remarkable, with the Islands one having such a lingering peaty aftertaste you could be forgiven for thinking that with one bite you are transported to a peat fire on Islay. The Highland and Speyside cakes are also excellent, although with less of a distinctive peatiness.

If you are making this cake with whisky connoisseurs in mind, then try it with an Islay malt; if you simply want a good whisky hit with no discernible smokiness, then use a Highland or Speyside.

MAKES 1 SUBSTANTIAL CAKE
300g/10^1/$_2$ oz raisins
300g /10^1/$_2$ oz currants
100g/3^1/$_2$ oz mixed peel
350ml/12 fl oz malt whisky
150g/5^1/$_2$ oz butter, softened
150g/5^1/$_2$ oz dark muscovado sugar
3 large free-range eggs
200g/7 oz self-raising flour
2 teaspoons mixed spice
40g/1^1/$_2$ oz ground almonds

1 Soak all the fruit in the whisky overnight. (If it is really warm – unlikely as it is in Scotland – I put it into the fridge overnight then bring back to room temperature well before mixing.)

2 Preheat the oven to 170°C/325°F/ Gas 3 and line a 22–23cm /8^1/$_2$–9 in deep cake tin. (I line the sides of the tin with high lining paper, which protects the surface from burning.)

3 Cream the butter and sugar together until soft and light.

Add the eggs one by one then tip in all the fruit and whisky.

4 Sift in the flour and spice, add the almonds and combine well.

5 Spoon into the prepared tin. Bake for 1^3/$_4$–2 hours, or until a skewer inserted into the centre comes out clean. (It is a good idea to cover the top loosely with foil towards the end of cooking, to prevent the fruit that pokes out from burning.) Transfer to a wire rack and leave until completely cold before removing from the tin.

Raspberries – and Other Berries and Currants

My thoughts on tasting the first raspberry of the season are not of melba sauce, clotted cream or jam, but of luggies, dreels, and dyed red fingernails. For I was one of that happy band of berry pickers who were paid a paltry sum of money to pick berries all day long in sun, rain or wind, for the whole month of July. In Angus and Perthshire, summer holidays and berries were inextricably linked. Hordes of schoolchildren would walk, cycle or catch a bus to 'go to the berries'. It was a way of life and the irritating scratches and red-stained T-shirts were part and parcel.

On arrival at the fruit farm in the morning, we would collect our buckets (called 'luggies') and tie them round our waists with string. Then we would be dispatched to the fields – mainly of raspberries but, if you were unlucky, you were off on the back of a tractor over bumpy terrain to blackcurrant bushes, which were impossible to pick without squashing into jam between eager fingers. Gooseberries were also unpopular as they were prickly and tasted sour. No, best of all were raspberries, as your back didn't ache as it did with strawberries; you were sheltered from the worst vagaries of the weather by the high leafy canes, and because of the length of the rows (called 'dreels') you could have deep or meaningless conversations with your fellow pickers if the appeal of devouring more forbidden fruit began to pall.

The trouble with raspberries was that they tasted so good, most of the ones I picked never made it into my luggie. My smile must have been rather unsightly, with recalcitrant little seeds sticking between every tooth. Raspberry pips are, perhaps surprisingly, of great historic significance as they were found in glacial deposits in the Scottish Lowlands – proof that the wild berry has been with us for quite some time. Scotland has retained its claim as the world's best raspberry grower because of the cool, moist climate. More recent varieties to look out for are Glen Ample and Glen Rosa (mid-season berries) and Glen Magna, a dark red, late cultivar. These days, raspberry canes are spine-free, so itinerant pickers need not worry about scratches and cuts as we did. Besides, half of the industrial fruit picking is now done by machine.

The tayberry (a cross between a raspberry and blackberry) was under development while I was picking in Invergowrie (where my Auntie Bette lived) near Dundee, at what is now the Scottish Crop Research Institute, the world's largest producer of raspberries and blackcurrants. The tayberry's sister, the tummelberry (developed from another seedling from the same crop) is less aromatic than the tayberry and hardier.

At the end of a long berry-picking day there was a stream of weary children struggling with their luggies to the weighing area. Some managed to pick pound upon pound of berries in a day; I hated them. Others contrived to cheat by concealing stones or liquids in the bottom of their luggies; I rather envied their audacity. Others – myself included – just smiled that seedy smile and resolved that next day more berries would go into the luggie, not into the mouth.

At a baking demonstration a few years ago in the remote north-east corner of Scotland, as I layered up some deep crimson raspberries into my dark muscovado brownies I told the guests about all the extras I put into brownies, from pears with cardamom to white chocolate with cranberries. But possibly my favourite – certainly in summer when the local fruit is ripe and juicy – are raspberries. As I finished spreading the thick gloop of luscious raw brownie batter over the raspberries, I looked up at my audience of local

Highland ladies and noticed a hand shoot up. A question perhaps about how much baking powder I had added to the batter? Or whether frozen berries are suitable to use in winter? No, the question from this respectable-looking middle-aged lady in a kilt was unexpected.

'Sue,' she said, 'do you ever put cannabis in your brownies?'

Not usually lost for words, I momentarily faltered but then, all too aware there was a journalist in my audience, decided to deflect rather than challenge. ('No, but do you?' was, oh so tempting.) I therefore cross-referred to a recipe for hashish fudge in the *Alice B. Toklas Cookbook*, from her time living in Paris with Gertrude Stein – all the while trying to concentrate on my own totally licit brownies.

Afterwards, as we chatted over tea and scones, I spotted the bekilted questioner and asked if I might inquire if she spoke from experience. She chuckled and said she couldn't possibly comment, but she had recently had a visit from the local police asking if they could check out the tomato plants in her greenhouse.

Sue with two ice creams (don't ask) and Carol and Lynda, Edinburgh, 1959

Brora Raspberry Jam

Mary Coghill from Brora makes the best raspberry jam in Christendom. And the secret of her brightly coloured, fresh-tasting raspberry jam is given below: it is only boiled with the sugar for 1 minute then beaten madly for 4. By this stage you will be cursing me and wondering if this will ever set, but believe me, it will. And when it does, you will agree it is the best jam ever, not only tasting fresh and fruity but also looking so bright it resembles freshly picked berries, not boiled jam.

Follow the timings here precisely and don't forget to don rubber gloves when beating the jam, as if it splatters it will burn.

MAKES ABOUT 4–5 JARS
1kg/2 lb 4 oz raspberries
1kg/2 lb 4 oz preserving sugar (not 'jam sugar', which has added pectin)

1 Place the berries in a large preserving pan (or heavy-based saucepan) over a low heat. Stir occasionally as they release their juices, about 10 minutes, then increase to high and boil on a rolling boil for 2 minutes.

2 Lower the heat to medium, stir in the sugar and, stirring often, allow the sugar to dissolve, which takes at least 10 minutes. Once dissolved, it will no longer feel gritty.

3 Increase the heat to high and once boiling rapidly, boil for 1 minute, then remove from the heat. Beat like mad (ensuring you are protected from any splatters) for 4 minutes, then pot in warm, sterilised jars. Once cool, seal and label. (To sterilise jars before potting, wash them well then dry in a low oven. Or if you have a dishwasher, put them through a cycle then, once thoroughly dry, microwave on High for 1½–2 minutes to warm.)

Raspberry Curd

This exquisitely coloured curd is fabulous made with fresh raspberries during the summer but I have made it out of season with frozen. It is wonderful on hot scones, crumpets or pancakes, but can also be used to fill a sponge cake. Or you can convert it into a delicious yogurt ice cream by mixing one jar with 500g/1 lb 2 oz Greek yogurt and freezing.

MAKES ABOUT 2–3 JARS
175g/6 oz raspberries (if using frozen, pat thoroughly dry)
100g/3¹/₂ oz unsalted butter, diced
200g/7 oz golden granulated sugar
the grated zest of 1 unwaxed lemon
150ml/5 fl oz/¹/₄ pint freshly squeezed lemon juice
3 large free-range eggs, beaten

1 Purée the berries in a food processor.

2 Place the butter, sugar, lemon zest and juice in a microwaveable bowl and cook, uncovered, on High for 4–5 minutes, stirring once, until the butter is melted and the sugar dissolved. Remove and cool for a couple of minutes. (Alternatively put the bowl over a pan of simmering water and stir all the time until thick.)

3 Place a plastic sieve over the bowl and push the eggs and berry purée through the sieve, so that any blobby bits of egg white and all raspberry pips remain in the sieve. Stir the buttery mixture as you push the berry mixture through the sieve.

4 Stir well then return to the microwave (or to the pan of simmering water) and cook for 5–6 minutes, removing every 1 minute and whisking madly until it thickens (otherwise it will scramble), ensuring you get into all the corners. It should have the consistency of lightly whipped cream and will firm up on cooling.

5 Spoon into warm, sterilised jars. (You will probably have a little left over – not enough to pot so, time to sit down with a cup of tea, buttered warm scone, or hot toast, and fresh raspberry curd.) Cover when completely cold and refrigerate. You can keep the curd for up to 4 weeks. (To sterilise jars, wash them in hot soapy water, rinse then dry in a low oven. Or if you have a dishwasher, put them through a dishwasher cycle then microwave on High for 1¹/₂ minutes.)

White Chocolate, Almond and Raspberry Cake with Raspberry Frosting and White Chocolate Drizzle

This mixture can also be made as cup cakes (it will make eight); bake for half the time then ice as for the cake.

SERVES 8

100g/3¹/₂ oz quality white chocolate (I like Green & Black's)
150g/5¹/₂ oz unsalted butter, softened
150g/5¹/₂ oz golden caster sugar
2 large free-range eggs
100g/3¹/₂ oz self-raising flour, sifted
a pinch of salt
50g/1³/₄ oz ground almonds
200g/7 oz raspberries
200g/7 oz golden icing sugar, sifted

1 Preheat the oven to 180°C/350°F/Gas 4 and base-line and butter a deep 18cm/7 in cake tin. Melt the chocolate over a pan of hot water. Beat the butter and caster sugar until fluffy then stir in the eggs one by one. Fold in the flour, salt and the almonds, then, once thoroughly combined, stir in most of the melted chocolate (you need to leave about 1 tablespoon to drizzle).

2 Tip into the prepared tin. Take 100g/3¹/₂ oz raspberries and poke these into the surface all over. Very gently smooth over with a spatula so the batter almost covers the berries. Do not worry if some poke out.

3 Bake in the oven for about 45 minutes, covering loosely with foil for the last 10 minutes. Test for readiness by inserting a wooden cocktail stick; it should come out clean.

4 Invert on to a wire rack to cool. Purée the remaining raspberries then push them through a sieve to eliminate the pips. Beat in the icing sugar until smooth. Once the cake is cool, spread the icing over the top. Re-melt the chocolate if necessary then drizzle over the top in zigzags or straight lines.

Fresh Raspberry Paradise Slice

I have adapted that great childhood favourite of mine, Paradise Slice, from Campbell's Bakery in Crieff. The traditional recipe has a layer of raspberry jam between pastry base and crunchy, fruity, coconut-frangipane topping. But I have used fresh berries to add a wonderful tang that contrasts well with the fabulously sweet topping – and also adds a welcome freshness.

You can, however, out of the raspberry season, use home-made raspberry jam: simply leave out the extra 1 tablespoon rice flour, smear about 6 heaped tablespoons best jam over the part-baked pastry then top as below. Both are divine, but it is the jam one that takes me directly back to my childhood in the most Proustian way.

MAKES 16–20 SLICES

150g/5^1/$_2$ oz rice flour, plus 1 heaped tablespoon

300g/10^1/$_2$ oz fresh raspberries, or 6 heaped tablespoons raspberry jam

250g/9 oz golden caster sugar

75g/2^3/$_4$ oz ground almonds

75g/2^3/$_4$ oz desiccated coconut

200g/7 oz butter, softened

2 large free-range eggs

250g/9 oz sultanas

100g/3^1/$_2$ oz undyed glacé cherries, halved

FOR THE PASTRY

200g/7 oz plain flour, sifted

50g/1^3/$_4$ oz ground almonds

25g/1 oz golden caster sugar

125g/4^1/$_2$ oz butter, diced

1 large free-range egg

1 For the pastry, place the flour, almonds and sugar in a food processor, combine briefly then add the butter and whiz until it resembles bread-crumbs. Slowly add the egg through the feeder tube, stopping the machine the minute it starts to form clumps. Alternatively, rub in the flour and butter mixture by hand and stir in the egg.

2 Lightly butter a 23 x 33cm/9 x 13 in Swiss roll tin. Bring the dough together with your hands, wrap in clingfilm and chill for 30 minutes or so then roll out to fit the prepared tin. Prick all over and chill well, preferably overnight.

3 Preheat the oven to 200°C/400°F/ Gas 6 and bake the pastry for 15 minutes. Remove and cool briefly. Sprinkle over 1 heaped tablespoon rice flour, then top with the raspberries. (Alternatively, omit the rice flour and spread with raspberry jam.) Lower the oven temperature to 180°C/350°F/Gas 4.

4 Place the sugar, almonds and coconut in a food processor, whiz briefly then add the butter. Process until combined, then add the eggs and 150g/5½ oz rice flour, process quickly then stir in the dried fruit. Alternatively, rub the butter into the mixture by hand and add the eggs, rice flour and dried fruit. Spoon carefully over the berries (or jam), smoothing the surface.

5 Bake for about 40–45 minutes, or until golden brown and set. Remove to a wire rack, cool then cut into slices.

Raspberry Ripple Yogurt Ice Cream

There are many pictures of me as a child with an ice cream cone (sometimes two!) drizzled with raspberry sauce and bought from the ice cream vans that came round our streets. There were those who preferred an ice cream wafer (and squashers with snowballs in between the wafer/ice cream combo), but for me it was that unique combination of whiter than white Italo-Scots ice cream with a squoosh of raspberry sauce on top that simply said, summertime.

SERVES 4
500g/1 lb 2 oz Greek yogurt (traditional, not Greek-style)
85g/3 oz golden icing sugar, sifted
150g/5½ oz raspberries

1 Whiz the yogurt and 60g/2¼ oz icing sugar in a food processor or blender until smooth then tip into a shallow freezer container. Cover and freeze for an hour then remove and whisk madly.

2 Meanwhile, purée the berries in a processor or blender with the remaining sugar then push through a sieve to eliminate any pips.

3 Smooth the surface of the ice cream then drizzle in the purée to form zigzags. Using a long skewer, 'feather' the surface to give a rippled effect. Cover and re-freeze for a couple of hours or until firm. Bring to room temperature before serving.

Blackcurrant and Bramble Cobbler with Oaty Streusel

This wonderful hot pudding can be made using other fruits: substitute blueberries or sliced plums for the blackcurrants but reduce the sugar by about half. You can also opt for just one of the toppings, but I prefer both.

This is a pud that cries out for a great dollop of crème fraîche or ice cream. Or, if you are a Scot, both.

SERVES 6

500g/1 lb 2 oz blackcurrants
75g/2³/₄ oz golden caster sugar
25g/1 oz cornflour dissolved in 2
    tablespoons cold water
250g/9 oz brambles (blackberries)

FOR THE COBBLER TOPPING

100g/3¹/₂ oz self-raising flour
75g/2³/₄ oz fine polenta
1 teaspoon baking powder
¹/₂ teaspoon cinnamon
a pinch of salt

50g/1³/₄ oz golden caster sugar
the grated zest and juice of 1
    unwaxed lemon
50g/1³/₄ oz butter, melted and cooled
    very slightly
75ml/2¹/₂ fl oz milk

FOR THE OATY STREUSEL

50g/1³/₄ oz plain flour
50g/1³/₄ oz porridge (rolled) oats
75g/2³/₄ oz butter, diced
50g/1³/₄ oz light muscovado sugar

1 Preheat the oven to 200°C/400°F/ Gas 6. Place the blackcurrants, sugar and 2 tablespoons water in a pan and slowly heat until the sugar dissolves, stirring. Increase the heat and add the cornflour mixture. Stir over a medium heat for 3 minutes, or until thickened. Mix in the brambles and tip into a medium-sized round ovenproof dish, then cool.

2 To make the cobbler topping, sieve the flour, polenta, baking powder, cinnamon and salt into a bowl then add the sugar and lemon zest. Stir in the lemon juice and melted butter then quickly stir in the milk. (Do not overwork the dough.)

3 To make the streusel, place the flour and oats in a bowl and rub in the butter until it resembles a crumble, then stir in the sugar.

4 Drop the cobbler mixture in six spoonfuls over the berries then scatter the oaty streusel all over. Bake for about 40 minutes, or until the fruit bubbles up and the cobbles are cooked through. (Check by gently easing one off with the top of a sharp knife and looking underneath.)

5 Cool for at least 10 minutes then serve warm.

Raspberry Chocolate Fudge Tart

This utterly divine recipe is based on Konditor & Cook's tart sold in their wonderful London bakeries: it is to die for. And my version here is not bad either!

Although the original recipe calls for all dark chocolate, I like a mixture of 150g/5$^1/_2$ oz dark chocolate with 70 per cent cocoa solids and 100g/3$^1/_2$ oz good milk chocolate (30–40 per cent cocoa solids). This mixture of chocolates makes the tart slightly less sharp.

It can be served with pouring cream or on its own, but don't forget: it is gloriously rich so small slices will do.

SERVES 8

140g/5 oz plain flour
15g/$^1/_2$ oz cocoa powder
90g/3$^1/_4$ oz butter, diced
40g/1$^1/_2$ oz golden caster sugar
1 large free-range egg yolk

FOR THE FILLING

150g/5$^1/_2$ oz fresh raspberries
250g/9 oz quality dark chocolate
   (or dark and milk, as above)
300ml/10 fl oz/$^1/_2$ pint double cream
50g/1$^3/_4$ oz butter
2 tablespoons liquid glucose

1 To make the pastry, sift the flour and cocoa into a food processor and add the butter and sugar. Whiz until the mixture resembles breadcrumbs then add the egg yolk and enough cold water, about $^1/_2$–1 teaspoon, to combine to a dough. Alternatively, rub in the flour and butter mixture by hand and stir in the egg yolk and water.

2 Bring the dough together with your hands, wrap in clingfilm then chill for an hour or so. Grease and flour a 23cm/9 in shallow tart tin and roll the pastry out to fit. Prick with a fork all over and chill well, preferably overnight.

3 Preheat the oven to 190°C/375°F/ Gas 5. Line the pastry case with foil, fill with baking beans, and bake blind for 15 minutes. Remove the foil and beans, and continue to bake for 5–10 minutes more, or until cooked through. Allow to cool.

4 To make the filling, scatter the raspberries over the cooled base. Break up the chocolate and place in a bowl. Place the remaining ingredients in a saucepan and heat very gently, without boiling or even bubbling, until the butter melts, then remove from the heat. Pour over the chocolate and whisk or stir well to combine to a smooth ganache. Pour this slowly over the base, covering all the berries. Leave to firm up a little for a couple of hours before serving. If refrigerated, remove to room temperature for an hour before serving.

Bramble and Chocolate Bread

This is so exquisite, it comes with a health warning: once out of the oven you must go for a walk, as it smells so scrumptious it is impossible to resist cutting into it while still hot. But it should only be cut when barely warm or cold.

I like to use dark chocolate for this but milk chocolate makes it slightly less bitter. A mixture of both is perhaps ideal for all palates.

SERVES 8

500g/1 lb 2 oz unbleached strong white flour, sifted
7g sachet of fast-action/easy-blend dried yeast
25g/1 oz golden caster sugar
1 level teaspoon salt
2 tablespoons sunflower oil
150g/5½ oz quality milk and/or dark chocolate, chopped
250g/9 oz brambles (blackberries)

1 Mix the flour, yeast and sugar in a bowl with the salt. Make a well in the centre and slowly pour in the oil and enough tepid water (about 300ml/10 fl oz/½ pint) to make a softish dough. (To have tepid water, mix two-thirds boiling water and one-third cold water.)

2 Using floured hands, bring the dough together and turn out on to a floured board then knead for 8–10 minutes, or until smooth, regularly sprinkling lightly with flour (I use a flour shaker). The dough should be soft and shiny-looking but not too sticky. Place in an oiled bowl and cover with oiled clingfilm. Leave somewhere warm for 1–2 hours.

3 Lightly oil a baking sheet. Punch down the dough and roll out to a rectangle about 38 x 28cm/15 x 11 in.

4 Scatter the chocolate and brambles over the long half then roll up along the long side to make a roly-poly about 38cm/15 in long.

5 Place this on the prepared baking sheet and cover loosely with oiled clingfilm then place somewhere warm. Leave to rise for about 45 minutes. Meanwhile, preheat the oven to 230°C/450°F/Gas 8. Remove the clingfilm, slash the top of the loaf five to six times and bake in the oven for about 20–25 minutes. Remove to a wire rack to cool until just warm before eating.

Honey

Zipped tightly into my bee-proof 'moonsuit' with netted helmet, I walked nervously towards the hives. It was a gloriously warm summer morning in the Borders and all I could see around me were two shades of heather (bell and ling) along the sides of the valley. The tranquil picture was interrupted only by the glimpse of a stoat as it darted from one clump of sedge to another. Then, rather like a scene from 'The Charge of the Flight Brigade', the bees broke loose as bee-keeper John Mellis lifted off the top of the hive. Out they swarmed. Soon climbing all over my suit and buzzing menacingly near my face, the bees seemed more than a little angry. As John explained later, how would you like it if you were going about your daily business when suddenly the entire roof of your house was lifted off? After John had been stung several times through his custom-made bee gloves, he cheerily remarked that 'stings are just a hazard of the job'. It was then I made the decision that, from that moment on, all I intend to do is eat the product of those angry bees' toil; the potentially dangerous part I would leave to dedicated craft honey producers like John. And while I recovered at a safe distance with a comforting cup of tea, doorstep of bread and some of John's luscious honey, he explained how the hive works and how honey is actually made.

There is usually one queen bee and some 40,000–50,000 worker bees to one hive in summertime. The queen, having been fed on royal jelly for the first few days of her life, lives for up to 5 years; the workers for a mere 6 weeks. To prevent the Queen from simply flying away with her entire colony of bees, one of her wings is clipped. And as John showed me how he clips a queen bee's wing, I once again thought, rather him than me.

Within the complex hierarchy of each colony, the female bees are given specific roles – foragers, nurses, scouts, guards and even undertakers. The drones (the only males) account for only some 100 per hive, but I feel sure even these non-working males had joined the rest of the hive to buzz threateningly around my head that day up the glen.

Nectar has around 40–60 per cent moisture, and to reduce this to honey, the forager bees who collect nectar – flying for up to 3 miles from the hive – pass it on to the hive bees who carry it on the end of their tongues until the air flow reduces the moisture level to around 18–20 per cent. This becomes thicker and more concentrated and it is now honey. The wooden frames of honeycomb removed by John are taken to his home in Dumfriesshire where the honey is extracted centrifugally – or in the case of heather honey by a complex structure of needles because of its gel-like consistency. Unlike the runny texture of most honeys, the consistency of heather honey means that to form a set honey it needs the addition of some other honey such as rape (most honeys in this country are from rape) which granulates more quickly. But I recommend you try pure heather honey: it is a revelation.

As are the nuances of flavour within various honeys. At a honey tasting, I compared a delicate springtime sycamore-and-hawthorn honey with a summer bell heather and lime, both of which were totally different.

Having done the hive adventure, I now truly appreciate the effort that goes into honey as I lather it on to oatcakes or drizzle it over pancakes. That effort is made not only by the bees but also by dedicated bee-keepers like John Mellis, who told me on the drive home that, on reflection, it was probably not a good idea for my first visit to go to hives on heather, as bees become increasingly aggressive on heather moors. Ah well, I survived, got the T-shirt – and now I'll just keep taking the honey.

Hare with Claret, Honey and Juniper

In centuries past in Scotland, hare was often cooked either simply in soups or stews or in more elaborate dishes such as 'ragous' and 'pyes'. A sauce that used to accompany roast hare I found in Mrs Johnston's 1740 cookery book includes spinach, parsley, sorrel, vinegar, butter and claret. Her 'hare pye' recipe contains hare, bacon, currants, raisins, butter and again claret.

And so the hare-claret theme is by no means new; but my recipe also incorporates some heather honey, as I like to think of a Scottish hare bounding across the heather moors, perhaps taking in some juniper bushes en route.

This delicious recipe is good served with mashed potatoes and parsnips or with pappardelle in the style of the Tuscan recipe, *sugo di lepre*. It reheats well, so can be made in advance. Diced venison is also suitable, if you cannot find hare.

SERVES 4–6

about 2 tablespoons extra virgin olive oil
1 onion, peeled and chopped
2 celery sticks, chopped
about 1kg/2 lb 4 oz hare joints or diced meat
2 tablespoons plain flour
350ml/12 fl oz claret
2 tablespoons juniper berries, crushed in a mortar and pestle
about 1 heaped tablespoon honey (preferably heather honey)
salt and freshly ground black pepper

1 Preheat the oven to 150°C/300°F/ Gas 2. Heat the oil in a flameproof casserole and then gently fry the onion and celery until soft. Remove with a slotted spoon and increase the heat. Add a splash more oil if there is little left.

2 Dust the hare in the flour then add to the casserole and brown all over. Return the vegetables to the casserole and increase the heat. Add the claret, juniper, and salt and pepper. Once boiling, cover and transfer to the oven for 1 hour. Remove from the oven, stir in the honey and then re-cover and cook for a further 1–1¹/₂ hours. Check the seasoning and add more honey if you think it needs more sweetness. Serve piping hot.

Rhubarb, Honey and Oat Cobbler

This delicious recipe was inspired by one I saw in a magazine but I have introduced honey and vanilla, both of which go so well with rhubarb. The gloriously pink rhubarb is cooked to spoon tenderness, and topped with the crunchiest of oaty cobbles. Yum!

SERVES 4–6

500g/1 lb 2 oz young rhubarb, trimmed and chopped
4 tablespoons runny honey
2 tablespoons light muscovado sugar
2 teaspoons vanilla extract
150g/5¹/₂ oz whole rolled oats
100ml/3¹/₂ fl oz double cream

1 Preheat the oven to 180°C/350°F/Gas 4. Place the rhubarb in an ovenproof dish with 2 tablespoons honey, the sugar and vanilla. Cover and bake in the oven for 20 minutes then remove. Leave the oven on.

2 Mix the oats with the remaining 2 tablespoons honey and the cream.

3 Drop spoonfuls of the oat mixture on top of the rhubarb in great blobs. Bake in the oven, uncovered, for about 30 minutes, or until tender and crunchy golden on top. Serve warm with crème fraîche.

Chocolate-smeared baby Sue, 1956

Nougat Ice Cream Bombe

This can be made several days in advance.

SERVES 6–8

50g/1³/₄ oz toasted, blanched almonds, roughly chopped or flaked
50g/1³/₄ oz toasted hazelnuts, roughly chopped or flaked
500ml/18 fl oz milk
3 tablespoons honey
4 large free-range egg yolks
75g/2³/₄ oz golden caster sugar
250ml/9 fl oz mascarpone
200g/7 oz undyed (natural) glacé cherries, halved
100g/3¹/₂ oz dried pineapple/papaya/mango, diced

1 If you don't have toasted and blanched almonds or toasted hazelnuts, first blanch the almonds by putting them into a small bowl and pouring over boiling water to cover. Leave to cool, strain off the water and squeeze the skins from the almonds. Toast the almonds and hazelnuts by spreading them on to a foil-lined baking tray and placing this under a preheated medium grill. Toast for about 5 minutes, turning them regularly until golden brown. Remove and allow to cool. Rub off the hazelnut skins by putting a handful into a tea towel and rubbing briskly. Roughly chop or flake the nuts.

2 To make the custard, place the milk and honey in a heavy-based saucepan and slowly bring to the boil.

3 Meanwhile, using an electric whisk, whisk the eggs yolks and sugar together until pale and creamy, about 2–3 minutes.

4 Gradually pour the hot milk over the egg mixture, whisking all the time. Then return to the pan and cook gently over a low heat, whisking constantly, until it thickens slightly, about 6–8 minutes. Do not allow it to boil.

5 Once thick enough to coat the back of a wooden spoon, remove and place in a basin of cold water. Stir occasionally until cold.

6 Once the custard is cold, add the mascarpone and whisk well until smooth. Stir in the nuts and fruit until well combined. Tip into a 1 litre/1³/₄ pint pudding basin. Cover with clingfilm and place in a freezer for at least 6 hours.

7 To serve, dip the basin briefly into hot water and invert on to a serving dish, then leave in the refrigerator for at least 30 minutes to soften up a little. Serve in slices.

Honey and Pine Nut Tart

This is based on a tart served in one of my favourite coffee shops, Edinburgh's Glass & Thompson, where you can have some wonderful home-baking with your latte. They use orange blossom honey, but I use regular runny honey and add some orange zest and orange flower water for flavour.

SERVES 8

200g/7 oz plain flour
25g/1 oz golden icing sugar
125g/4¹/₂ oz butter, diced

FOR THE FILLING

100g/3¹/₂ oz butter, softened
100g/3¹/₂ oz golden caster sugar
2 large free-range eggs
5–6 tablespoons runny honey, about 175g/6 oz
1 tablespoon orange flower water
the grated zest of 1 small orange
200g/7 oz pine nuts (toasted until pale golden and nutty smelling)

1 Sift the flour and sugar into a food processor then add the butter and process briefly. Add just enough cold water so that you can bring it together to a dough, about 50ml/ 2 fl oz. Alternatively, rub in the flour and butter mixture by hand and stir in the egg. Wrap in clingfilm and chill for an hour or so.

2 Roll out to fit a shallow, 24cm/9¹/₂ in tart tin with a removable base. Chill for several hours or overnight.

3 Preheat the oven to 200°C/400°F/ Gas 6. Line the pastry case with foil and fill with baking beans, and then blind bake for 15 minutes. Remove the foil and beans, and continue to cook for 10 minutes, then remove. Reduce the oven to 170°C/325°F/Gas 3.

4 To make the filling, beat the butter and sugar together until fluffy, then beat in the eggs one by one. Add the honey, orange flower water and orange zest, and beat everything together, then gently fold in the pine nuts.

5 Tip this into the pastry case and bake for about 40 minutes, or until golden brown and just set. Leave until cold before cutting.

Honey and Rhubarb Muffins

This recipe was inspired by one I found in an Amish cookbook, full of glorious Shoofly Pie, Friendship Bread and Morning Glory Muffins. Baking is a strongpoint of the Amish heritage and these do not disappoint.

Oh, and before you say, 'She's missed out the eggs' – there are none!

MAKES 8 AMERICAN-SIZE OR 12 REGULAR MUFFINS

50g/1³/₄ oz toasted hazelnuts, chopped
50g/1³/₄ oz light muscovado sugar
4 tablespoons runny honey
100ml/3¹/₂ fl oz sunflower oil
100ml/3¹/₂ fl oz natural yogurt
100g/3¹/₂ oz young rhubarb, finely diced
200g/7 oz self-raising flour (I like one-third wholemeal, two-thirds regular)
¹/₂ teaspoon baking powder
¹/₂ teaspoon cinnamon

1 Preheat the oven to 200°C/400°F/Gas 6. If you don't have toasted hazelnuts, spread them on to a foil-lined baking tray and place this under a preheated medium grill. Toast for about 5 minutes, turning them regularly until golden brown. Remove and allow to cool. Remove the skins by putting a handful into a tea towel and rubbing briskly. Chop the nuts.

2 Beat together the sugar, honey, oil and yogurt, then stir in the rhubarb and nuts.

3 Sift in the flour, baking powder and cinnamon, mix together and then spoon into eight large muffin cases (or 12 regular) set in a muffin tin. Bake in the oven for 20 minutes, or until risen and golden. Eat warm.

Apple Sour-cream Cake with Honey Drizzle

This is good with afternoon tea.

MAKES 1 CAKE
450g/1 lb Cox's or Golden Delicious apples, peeled and sliced
150g/5¹/₂ oz butter, softened
the grated zest of 1 unwaxed lemon
150g/5¹/₂ oz golden caster sugar
1 large free-range egg
150ml/5 fl oz/¹/₄ pint soured cream
150g/5¹/₂ oz self-raising flour, sifted
3 tablespoons honey

1 Preheat the oven to 180°C/350°F/ Gas 4 and butter an 18cm/7 in deep cake tin.

2 Place the apple slices in a frying pan with 25g/1 oz butter and very gently sauté for 8–10 minutes, or until almost soft. Remove from the heat and stir in the lemon zest. Cool a little.

3 Beat the remaining butter with the sugar until smooth. Beat in the egg then the soured cream. Once smooth, fold in the flour and the apples. Turn into the prepared tin, smoothing the top. Bake in the oven for 1–1 hour 5 minutes, or until cooked through. (Test with a cocktail stick inserted into the centre: it should come out clean.)

4 Remove to a wire rack and carefully remove the side of the cake tin but keep the base on the cake. Transfer with the base to a serving plate.

5 Heat the honey in a small pan and, once bubbling, drizzle slowly over the cake. Allow to cool before serving. (Remove the cake from the base, if you prefer.)

Butter and Cream

Meg McMillan goes into her farmhouse kitchen and dons her rubber gloves. But not to embark on a mound of washing-up; rather, to make shortbread. Because she has hot hands and shortbread (like pastry) requires cold hands, she has to run the gloves under the cold tap, dry them, then quickly set to. What might seem like a palaver is more than worth it. For Meg's shortbread is the best.

But this shortbread-baking skill is not innate. Hers is not a farming background (she is a maths teacher). When she married Euan, though, who farms sheep and cattle near Traquair in the Borders, over three decades ago, she had to learn – and quickly. She has therefore perfected not only the results but she has also made the entire shortbread-baking technique into an art.

On the morning I arrived, there was a problem. She had changed the hour of day she bakes from evening to early morning and this meant, she insisted, the shortbread was not quite right. It tasted fabulous to me, but she said it was not the classic pale golden brown on top and underneath, and cooked through in the middle. She blamed the surge of electricity in their rural setting at different times of the day. With or without the imperatives of evening baking and rubber gloves, anyone can make Meg's shortbread, provided of course only the best ingredients are used. Once the butter and sugar is creamed – at length – the flour and cornflour are added slowly, then once this has come together, this dough is chilled. (The small proportion of cornflour not only gives the melting texture, it also helps lower the gluten.) Rubber gloves are then once more donned, the dough patted out into four circles to fit the tins, pricked and baked for no less, no more, than 45 minutes.

And so from home baked to commercial, I travelled north to Deans of Huntly. In rural Aberdeenshire, Huntly is where, back in 1975, Helen Dean decided to bake shortbread to raise money for the Huntly Pipe Band in which her husband was drum major. It was so popular that soon Helen opened her own small bakery and eventually, in 1992, moved to a purpose-built site. But the wonderful thing about this shortbread, as opposed to others that are mass-produced (prepared and baked in less than 40 minutes), in Huntly it is made in exactly the same way as home-made.

So just as the home baker brings the butter to room temperature before beating with the sugar, so the salted Scottish butter 'tempers' for a few hours before being mixed with sugar, then flour and cornflour are added and it is mixed 'just until it's ready'. According to the bakers, there is no specific time given; it is all judged by experience. It is then pressed into large baking trays and trimmed by hand, then the prickle dockers – rollers with large hedgehog-like prickles all over – are adeptly rolled back and forth to give the shortbread its characteristic pricks. There are also moulds for petticoat tails: the classic round of eight thin wedges with their prettily scalloped border. And then both shortbread trays and round petticoat tail moulds are baked.

And again, just like shortbread baked at home, it is baked long and slow, so there is no crisp outside with semi-raw inside, like some fast-baked commercial brands. It is evenly cooked, buttery and soft, and yet crisp outside.

So, there I was, all trussed up in white coat, matching hat and snood, watching the prickle dockers at work. But as I watched, I could hardly concentrate on anything apart from the aroma. Sweet, buttery, homely and utterly tantalising. Eat your heart out,

Charlie Bucket; nothing – not even an entire chocolate factory – could smell as alluring as warm, freshly baked shortbread.

The smell was not simply one of the most pleasing in the world, it was also a direct link back to my childhood, to those garden fêtes and church fairs in the endless summers of youth, where I would stand in long queues to buy tablet, home-made macaroon bars and shortbread. It is, for me, a taste of the past and yet, reassuringly, a taste of the present, for this is what good Scottish shortbread is all about: three basic ingredients, slowly mixed and then baked even more slowly. I am ashamed to confess, however, that I do not continue the adherence to slow food as I eat. With the speed of a prickle docker, I wolf down the exquisite buttery mouthfuls before pausing for breath, all the while thanking the Good Lord for one of Scotland's greatest culinary gifts to the world, shortbread.

Meg's Shortbread
Meg McMillan usually makes her shortbread with two-thirds butter and one-third margarine; I always prefer the pure flavour of all butter.

MAKES 16
175g/6 oz slightly salted butter, softened
85g/3 oz golden caster sugar, plus extra to sprinkle
175g/6 oz plain flour, sifted
55g/2 oz cornflour, sifted

1 Beat the butter and sugar together until really creamy and pale; this will take 4–5 minutes in a food mixer (double the time by hand).

2 Combine the flour and cornflour and add a tablespoonful at a time, only adding more when each spoonful is fully incorporated. When all is mixed in, beat hard for 1 minute (on full speed if using a mixer).

3 Bring the dough together with your hands and wrap in clingfilm. Refrigerate for 20 minutes or so, to firm a little. Meanwhile, preheat the oven to 150°C/300°F/Gas 2.

4 Cut into two pieces and pat each out into circles. Transfer to two 18cm/7 in lightly buttered tins. (Meg rolls the dough out on a board to the complete size of the tin and then inverts it into the tins from the board. I place the circle of dough – not quite the size of the tin – into the tins and push out gently to fit the edges.) Level the surface then prick all over with a fork.

5 Bake in the oven for 40–45 minutes (my oven takes 40; Meg's 45) until a pale golden brown. Remove the tins to a wire rack, cut each into eight triangles and sprinkle over some sugar. Leave for 15–20 minutes or so then remove from the tins while still a little warm but firm. Leave on a wire rack until cold.

Buttery Butteries

I have been fortunate enough to visit lots of craft bakers throughout Scotland and, in those where butteries were sold, my question was always, 'Why are butteries not made with butter?' Sandy Milne, from family bakers Fisher and Donaldson in St Andrews, said that it has never been traditional to use butter. It was always 'white fat' or lard, although original Aberdeen fishermen's rowies (Aberdonians refer to them as 'rowies'; elsewhere they are 'butteries') were made with butcher's dripping or lard. They had been 'designed' to last a long time, so the fishermen could eat them on long trips away at sea. At Asher's bakers in Nairn they are still made with lard, in the old-fashioned way and taste wonderful.

Sandy Milne, however, decided to do an all-butter batch for me and was so impressed (the flavour is incomparable), he has continued to bake them every day in his fabulous bakery: they cost his customers two pence more (sorry, St Andrews), but for that pure butter flavour, it is well worth it. This recipe is an adaptation of Sandy's and is utterly divine. These are a revelation.

They are the perfect accompaniment to soup, salad or cheese. You do not need to proffer butter for spreading on top as is the norm in Aberdeenshire; the butter is already there.

(This basic dough recipe is also versatile: once risen, you can shape into a loaf without adding the butter, then leave for a second rise before baking in a hot oven for about 25 minutes. Or you can add 2 tablespoons sugar to the risen dough, then cut into small pieces, roll into rounds, glaze with an egg, leave to rise and then bake in a hot oven for 15 minutes, or until golden and shiny; these are bridge rolls.)

MAKES 16

600g/1 lb 5 oz strong white flour
7g sachet fast-action/easy-blend dried yeast
1 level teaspoon sugar
2 teaspoons salt
200g/7 oz butter, softened
1 heaped teaspoon sea salt

1 Put the flour into a large bowl. Add the yeast, sugar and 2 teaspoons salt, and mix well. Add enough tepid water to combine to a dough, about 350ml/12 fl oz. Turn on to a board and knead for 7–8 minutes, or until smooth. Place in large bowl, cover and leave somewhere vaguely warm for a couple of hours, or until risen.

2 Punch down and roll out with your palms to form a rectangle. Cut the butter into three long slices. Add a third at a time, to a third of the bread dough. Then fold over and continue with the remaining thirds. It is a folding process, rather like puff pastry.

3 Now, either knead by pushing, folding and turning the dough until you can see the butter is incorporated. Or, if you prefer, using well-floured hands, chop in the fat by hand, with the blade of a blunt knife, a pastry scraper or the long edge of a palette knife. Once well combined, the dough will be slightly sticky. (You will need to flour your hands throughout this preparation.)

4 Cut into about 16 pieces and place these on a lightly floured (not buttered) large baking sheet. Shape them by pressing the front part of your floured hand (fingers only) on to each, so that they are flattened and dimpled with fingerprints with one stroke.

5 Sprinkle some sea salt over the top of each. Then cover with oiled clingfilm and leave to prove somewhere warm for another 30 minutes or so. Meanwhile, preheat the oven to 230°C/450°F/Gas 8.

6 Bake the butteries for about 20 minutes, or until crispy and golden. Remove to a wire rack to cool.

Craggy Date Shorties

This is an adaptation of a recipe by Alison Keeble who bakes wonderful cakes and tray bakes for Robertson's Butcher's Shop in Broughty Ferry. Mine is 'shorter' in texture – and also less deep than Alison's. These are delicious with an afternoon cup of tea.

MAKES ABOUT 24 SQUARES
375g/13 oz dried dates, stoned and chopped
25g/1 oz butter
the grated zest of 1 large orange
150ml/5 fl oz/¹/₄ pint fresh orange juice
1 teaspoon ground cinnamon
FOR THE SHORTBREAD
350g/12 oz butter
175g/6 oz golden caster sugar
400g/14 oz plain flour, sifted
a pinch of salt
100g/3¹/₂ oz cornflour, sifted
unrefined demerara sugar, to sprinkle

1 Preheat the oven to 150°C/300°F/ Gas 2 and butter a 23 x 33cm/9 x 13 in Swiss roll tin.

2 Place the dates, butter, orange zest, juice and cinnamon in a pan and bring to the boil. Lower the heat and simmer, uncovered, for about 5 minutes, or until the dates are soft. Remove from the heat and cool.

3 For the shortbread, beat the butter and caster sugar together until light and fluffy; this will take about 10 minutes. Gradually add the flour and salt. Combine very briefly, until it just comes together as a dough.

4 Tip two-thirds of this mixture into the prepared tin, pressing down, then top with the cooled date mixture, spreading it out evenly. Break the remaining shortbread mixture into nuggets and dot all over the dates, but do not press down (you want the craggy look, not the smooth, sophisticated look). Bake in the oven for 65–70 minutes, or until golden.

5 Sprinkle with demerara sugar and cut into squares while hot, then leave until cold before removing from the tin.

Orkney Fudge Cheesecake
Based on Julia's Café's Recipe

Because this is so fabulous, I have given two recipes. One is light and fluffy in texture and with a good hint of fudge, the other dense and creamy and seriously fudgy. The first is the one my husband adores and although I also love it, I would crawl over broken glass for a slab of the second one (Paul's recipe on the next page). During a two-day visit up to Orkney, I managed to eat this now hugely popular cheesecake three times (and some say my job is easy) and each time they were very different. (Locals reckon it has been a menu staple – rather like Sticky Toffee Pudding in the 1970s – for some 10 years.)

Orkney fudge is rich, buttery and creamy, and converts perfectly into a cheesecake: grated in Julia's recipe and melted in Paul's. Although both recipes are good eaten on the day they are made, I prefer both the day after, when the chopped fudge has had time to somehow become gooey and molten within the cheesecake filling. Heaven on earth!

Julia's Café is a charming little café in Stromness, birthplace of the poet legend George Mackay Brown. One of his most famous works is entitled 'Letters from Hamnavoe' after the town's traditional name.

In this recipe you can substitute tablet for the fudge, as it is equally easily grated.

SERVES 8

250g/9 oz Hobnobs (or other oaty biscuits), crushed
75g/2³/₄ oz butter, melted
200g/7 oz Philadelphia cream cheese
250g/9 oz Orkney fudge (or tablet)
600ml/20 fl oz/1 pint double cream, lightly whipped

1 Lightly butter a 24cm/9¹/₂ in springform cake tin. Make the base by combining the biscuits and butter, and pressing into the base of the prepared tin.

2 Beat the cream cheese until soft.

3 Grate 200g/7 oz of the fudge (I use my food processor), and tip into the cream cheese. Combine gently – folding in slowly – with the cream.

4 Chop the remaining fudge and scatter over the cheesecake base in the tin. Spoon the cream mixture over the top and cover. Chill for at least 6 hours before carefully decanting and serving in wedges.

Orkney Fudge Cheesecake Based on the Foveran Hotel Recipe

Paul Doull (who also taught me how to make barley bannocks) and his brother Hamish run the Foveran Hotel in St Ola, near Kirkwall, which has a fabulous view over Scapa Flow. This is yet another restaurant using local produce and with a nod towards traditional Orcadian recipes, such as bere bannocks. This cheesecake recipe, although modern, exemplifies all that is good on Orkney: natural dairy produce and a sweet smile of indulgence from the fudge.

SERVES 8

250g/9 oz Hobnobs (or other oaty biscuit), crushed
75g/2³/₄ oz butter, melted
300g/10¹/₂ oz Philadelphia cream cheese
250g/9 oz Orkney fudge
450ml/16 fl oz double cream, lightly whipped

1 Lightly butter a 24cm/9¹/₂ in springform cake tin. Make the base by combining the biscuits and butter, and pressing into the base of the prepared tin.

2 Beat the cream cheese until soft.

3 Melt 200g/7 oz of the fudge by placing in a bowl in the microwave for about 1 minute, or until soft (or in a pan over a very low heat), so that when you stir it becomes a soft paste. You do not want it to be hot, only warm. Stir in the cream cheese, beating until combined, then gently fold in the cream.

4 Chop the remaining fudge and add to the mixture, then spoon into the biscuit base, smoothing the top, and chill for least 6 hours before serving.

Manse Shortbread

I have adapted this recipe from one I found in Margaret Stewart's hand-written recipe book from 1799. Her abode was Erskine (near Glasgow) where her husband was minister (hence my name for this delicious crisp shortbread).

The addition of caraway seeds, nuts and zest was very commonplace in those days and resembles the Pitcaithly bannock, which was baked in a round, rather like shortbread petticoat tails.

MAKES ABOUT 24

225g/8 oz butter, slightly softened
100g/3½ oz golden caster sugar, plus extra to sprinkle
200g/7 oz plain flour, sifted
100g/3½ oz rice flour or ground rice
1 heaped teaspoon caraway seeds
40g/1½ oz finely chopped almonds
the grated zest of 1 small orange
a pinch of salt

1 Preheat the oven to 150°C/300°F/ Gas 2 and lightly butter a 23 x 33cm/ 9 x 13 in Swiss roll tin.

2 Soften the butter slightly then place in a food mixer or a large bowl with the sugar. Cream until pale; this will take at least 4–5 minutes using a food mixer or double that time if beaten by hand.

3 Sift in the flour and rice flour or ground rice and the flavourings. Add the salt and process very briefly – until just brought together. Do not overprocess.

4 Tip into the prepared tin. Using floured hands, press down all over to level the surface. Prick all over with a fork then bake for 40–45 minutes, or until uniformly a pale golden brown.

5 Shake over some sugar from a dredger then cut into squares or fingers. Leave for 5–10 minutes then carefully remove to a wire rack to cool completely.

Chocolate Caramel Wafers

There can be few people growing up in the late 1950s and the 1960s who do not remember with great fondness Tunnock's caramel wafers. I have been lucky enough to visit Tunnock's to see the famous wafers (and logs and tea cakes) being made. The smell was almost too much to bear as I watched large sheets of wafers sandwiched together with caramel, cut into fingers then dunked in glossy chocolate. I was surprised to learn that the caramel wafer was only 'invented' in 1952; to me and most fellow Scots they had been with us forever!

This unusual recipe – which bears a vague resemblance to Tunnock's fabulous wafers (although Tunnock's have five wafers and four caramel layers, unlike these which have three wafer and two caramel) – was given to me by Dawn Powell who, with her husband Robert, runs the Royal Marine Hotel in Brora, a haven of friendly warm welcome and superb food.

MAKES 15
115g/4 oz butter
200g/7 oz (half a regular tin) of condensed milk
2 tablespoons golden syrup
350g/12 oz good quality chocolate (I like about two-thirds milk; one-third dark)
15 (original) Ryvita crispbreads

1 Place the butter, condensed milk and golden syrup in a solid saucepan and very slowly bring to the boil, stirring. Once bubbling, stir constantly for about 5 minutes, or until a pale caramel colour. Remove from the heat and cool until warm, not hot.

2 Melt the chocolate in a heatproof shallow bowl (for easy dipping) over a pan of hot water.

3 To assemble, spread a thick layer of caramel on to a crispbread, top with another, then spread more caramel over that. Finish with a third crispbread. Continue until all the crispbreads and caramel are used up. Using a very sharp knife, cut each of the five into three. Using two forks, dip each in the chocolate then lay out on greaseproof paper on a board to set.

Plume Caike

This fabulous recipe is a combination of two very old ones, both beautifully written in flowery hand, in two books I was priveleged to see at the National Library of Scotland. One recipe is in an anonymous book from the late seventeenth or early eighteenth century which has an elaborate recipe for a 'plume caike' starting, 'Take 7 pounds of flower [*sic*]' then 'take a pynt of creame and two pounds of butter . . .' It also has 22 eggs in it so we are not talking small cakes! The other recipe is from Janet Maule's recipe book from 1701 and calls for 'a muchken of sweet cream' among other things. This second recipe I somehow feel an affinity with, as Janet lived in Panmure, which is beside Dundee, my hometown. And since I have traced my ancestors (my maiden name is Anderson) back to 1741 and to the town of Alyth (north of Dundee), I like to imagine my lot making something similar if they worked in the Big Houses, as my great-grandmother did.

There is one ingredient in Janet Maule's recipe that is very interesting: she stipulates adding 'a pound of corduidron'. According to food historian Colin Spencer, this is preserved quince, from a form of the old French *condoignac*. Although the English referred to it as 'chardquynce', Scots would have preferred the French to the English word. (This is before the full Union in 1707, remember!) So, I sometimes add chopped quince paste (membrillo) for even more flavour.

This cake, which has the same basic flavourings as the old recipes, is wonderfully moist, probably from the unusual addition of cream. It is one of the nicest fruit cakes I know; and so easy to make.

MAKES 1 LARGE CAKE

400g/14 oz self-raising flour, sifted
350g/12 oz currants
50g/1¾ oz raisins
50g/1¾ oz mixed peel
the grated zest of 1 unwaxed lemon
the grated zest of 1 small orange
75g/2¾ oz quince paste, diced (optional)
½ teaspoon ground cinnamon
¼ teaspoon freshly grated nutmeg
¼ teaspoon ground cloves
¼ teaspoon ground mace
a pinch of salt
250g/9 oz butter, softened
150g/5½ oz light muscovado sugar
3 large free-range eggs
100ml/3½ fl oz double cream
50ml/2 fl oz medium sherry

1 Preheat the oven to 170°C/325°F/ Gas 3 and line a 22cm/8¹/₂ in tin ensuring that the paper is above the rim.

2 Mix the flour, currants, raisins, mixed peel, citrus zest, quince paste (if using), spices and salt together in a large bowl. Beat the butter and sugar together until thoroughly creamed, then beat in the eggs one by one. Stir into the flour mixture with the cream and sherry.

3 Once well combined, spoon into the prepared tin. Bake for 1 hour then reduce the temperature to 150°C/300°F/Gas 2. Place a piece of foil loosely over the top and continue to bake for a further 1¹/₄ hours (2¹/₄ hours altogether). It is cooked when a skewer inserted into the centre comes out clean.

4 Remove to a wire rack to cool before removing from the tin.

Fairy Butter

I developed this from a recipe I found in Elizabeth Cleland's 1755 Edinburgh book. She advocates serving this as it is, in little heaps on plates, which must have been a fairly rich dessert, perhaps served with dainty biscuits and a glass of sweet wine. F. Marian McNeill suggests soaking some Naples biscuits in white wine then putting some fairy butter over them 'in heaps as high as it can be raised'.

I like it as a floral-tasting butter icing for chocolate cakes, with Christmas pudding instead of brandy butter, or dolloped on to hot pancakes such as the *Oatmeal Pancakes From 1755* on page 164.

MAKES 1 SMALL BOWLFUL
the yolks of 2 large hard-boiled free-range eggs
100g/3¹/₂ oz butter, softened
140g/5 oz icing sugar, sifted
1 tablespoon orange flower water

1 Beat the yolks and butter together.

2 When well amalgamated, stir in the sugar and flower water, beating until smooth.

Shortbread Toffee Crumble Ice Cream Bars

Oh my, this recipe is so good I can hardly bear to share it with you. But share I must, for I have been known to banish everyone else from the kitchen – unusually – to do the washing-up by myself, with the express intent to eat another slab of this divine pudding all on my own. It is not grown-up and it is not pretty. But as I said: my, is it good!

MAKES 8 MIGHTY BARS

450g/1 lb shortbread (plain and/or choc-chip), crushed
125g/4¹/₂ oz butter, melted
1.2– 1.3 litres/2–2¹/₄ pints best vanilla ice cream, softened very slightly
about ²/₃ 450g jar of dulce de leche (or about 300ml/10 fl oz/¹/₂ pint thick
    toffee sauce

1 Line a 28 x 18cm/11 x 7 in baking tin with double foil or baking parchment, leaving some overhanging.

2 Mix the crushed shortbread and butter, then tip just over half into the tin, smoothing it out. Pop in the freezer for about 15 minutes, or until firm.

3 Spread the ice cream over the base, smoothing the top. Freeze again for about 30 minutes, until set.

4 Warm the dulce de leche or toffee sauce until just pourable (but not hot) and slowly drizzle over the ice cream. Break up the remaining shortbread mixture with your fingers and sprinkle over the sauce, like a crumble topping. Freeze again until firm (at least 4 hours) then remove from the tin, using the foil. Cut into bars.

Anta Bars

This divine recipe is one I have adapted from something called 'Magic Bars' which I discovered at Anta Pottery Café near Tain in Ross-shire. Gill and Andrea who run the café bake daily for customers and this is one of their most popular tray bakes.

MAKES 20-24 BARS

140g/5 oz butter, melted
350g/12 oz digestive biscuits, crumbed
400g/14 oz tin of condensed milk
200g/7 oz good quality milk chocolate, coarsely chopped or in small chunks
175g/6 oz desiccated coconut

1 Preheat the oven to 180°C/350°F/ Gas 4 and lightly butter a 23 x 33cm/ 9 x 13 in Swiss roll tin.

2 Mix the butter and biscuits together and spread into the prepared tin, pressing down to level.

3 Slowly pour over the tin of condensed milk, trying to leave a tiny margin around the edges so that it does not stick to the sides.

4 Scatter over the chocolate, evenly distributing it over the surface.

5 Finally, top with the coconut and pat down with the palms of your hands to ensure it is compact.

6 Bake in the oven for about 20 minutes, or until golden brown. Cool before cutting into bars.

Clotted Cream Cranachan

Although clotted cream is traditionally a West Country dish, I have found it in Elizabeth Cleland's 1755 Edinburgh book. There she includes a recipe for 'clouted cream' flavoured with rose water and sugar.

Clotted cream is made by 'scalding' and cooling milk in a specific process that makes the cream 'clot'. Brenda Leddy, who has been making her divine clotted cream at Stichill near Kelso for 20 years from her herd of 150 Jersey cows, explained that, to make it in the traditional way, you must first leave the milk out overnight. Then you heat it very gently in a bain marie for some five hours until the characteristic crust forms. It is then left in the cool larder overnight again before being skimmed and left once more all night. This process might seem long and laborious, but it is crucial for both flavour and texture.

Brenda and her daughter go to five Farmers' Markets a month and invariably sell out, which means that regular bedtime on Farmers' Market days is 3 a.m., once she has finished potting cream and labelling butter and cheese. At least she leaves the 5.30 a.m. milking to her daughter, while allowing herself a lie in until 6 a.m. I imagine her dreams are of dewy-eyed Jersey cows and golden, crusty clotted cream.

SERVES 4–6

350g/12 oz clotted cream
75g/2³⁄₄ oz whole rolled oats
75g/2³⁄₄ oz light muscovado sugar
2 tablespoons malt whisky
runny honey, to taste
500g/1 lb 2 oz berries (brambles, raspberries, strawberries)

1 Tip the cream into a bowl and stir.

2 Place the oats and sugar on a sheet of foil then place under a hot grill. Watch them constantly, removing and shaking about or forking through every 10–20 seconds or so. After a couple of minutes, the sugar will have caramelised and the oats will be golden. Do not overcook or they will burn – and remember to watch them like a hawk.

3 Remove and leave to cool. Break up the crunchy oats loosely between your fingers as you add them to the cream. Add the whisky, and honey to taste. Stir to combine, tip into a serving bowl and chill well. Serve with berries – and a drizzle of honey.

Useful Addresses

SCOTLAND'S TOURIST BOARD
Visit Scotland, Thistle House
Beechwood Park North
Inverness IV2 3ED
Tel 0845 2255121
www.visitscotland.com

**SCOTTISH ASSOCIATION
   OF MASTER BAKERS**
Atholl House
4 Torphichen Street
Edinburgh EH3 8JQ
Tel 0131 2291401
www.samb.co.uk

ARBROATH SMOKIES
R. R. Spink and Sons
Kirkton Industrial Estate
Arbroath DD11 3RD
Tel 01241 872023
www.rrspink.com

ASPARAGUS AND SEA KALE
A.H. & H.A. Pattullo
Eassie Farm, by Glamis
Tayside, DD8 1SG
Tel 01307 840303

AYRSHIRE BACON
Ramsay of Carluke
22 Mount Stewart Street
Carluke ML8 5ED
Tel 01555 772277
www.ramsayofcarluke.co.uk

BEEF
Donald Russell
Harlaw Road
Inverurie
Aberdeenshire AB51 4FR
Tel 01467 629666
www.donaldrusselldirect.com

BEREMEAL
Barony Mills, Birsay
Orkney KW17 2LY
Tel 01856 721309
www.birsay.org.uk

BLACK PUDDING
Stornoway black pudding
Charles Macleod Butcher
Ropewood Park
Stornoway HS1 2LB
Tel 01851 702445
www.charlesmacleod.co.uk

AND
Robert Grant Butcher
Main Street
Golspie KW10 6TG
Tel 01408 633246
AND
Donaldsons of Orkney
38 Albert Street
Kirkwall, Orkney KW15 1HQ
Tel 01856 872641

**BREAD, OLIVE OIL, HERBS
   AND MUCH MORE**
Valvona & Crolla Ltd
19 Elm Row
Edinburgh EH7 4AA
Tel 0131 5566066
www.valvonacrolla.com

FARMHOUSE CHEESE
Iain Mellis Cheesemonger
30a Victoria Street
Edinburgh EH1 2JW
Tel 0131 2266215
AND
492 Great Western Road
Glasgow G12 8EW
Tel 0141 3398998
www.ijmellischeesemonger.com

CLOTTED CREAM
Garden Cottage Farm, Stichill
Kelso, Roxburghshire TD5 7TL
Tel 01573 470263

GAME
Highland Game, Baird Avenue
Dryburgh Industrial Estate
Dundee DD2 3TN
Tel 01382 827088
www.highlandgame.com

HAGGIS
Macsween of Edinburgh
Bilston Glen
Loanhead EH20 9LZ
Tel 0131 4402555
www.macsween.co.uk

**HAGGIS, SHETLAND LAMB
   AND SAUSAGES**
Crombie's of Edinburgh
97 Broughton Street
Edinburgh EH1 3RZ
Tel 0131 5570111
www.sausages.co.uk

HERBS
Scotherbs
Kingswell, Longforgan
near Dundee DD2 5HJ
Tel 01382 360642
www.scotherbs.co.uk

HERRING
The Orkney Herring Company Ltd
Garson Food Park
Stromness
Orkney KW16 3JU
Tel 01856 850514
www.orkneyherring.com

HONEY
John Mellis
Cleuch House, Auldgirth
Dumfries DG2 0TP
Tel 01848 331280

KALE
East Coast Organics
24 Bogg Holdings
Pencaitland
East Lothian EH34 5BD
Tel 01875 340227

**LORNE SAUSAGE, BEEF,
   LAMB AND SCOTCH PIES**
Robertson's the Butcher
234 Brook Street
Broughty Ferry
Dundee DD5 2AH
Tel 01382 739277

MALT WHISKIES
Royal Mile Whiskies
379 High Street
Edinburgh EH1 1PW
Tel 0131 6226255
www.royalmilewhiskies.com

OATMEAL
The Oatmeal of Alford
Montgarrie Mill
Alford
Aberdeenshire AB33 8AP
Tel 01975 562209
www.oatmealofalford.com
AND
Hamlyns Oatmeal
Grampian Oats
Boyndie, Banff AB45 2LR
Tel 01261 843330
www.hamlynsoats.co.uk

OYSTERS
Islay Oysters
Craigens, Gruinart
Isle of Islay
Tel 01496 850256
www.islay-oysters.co.uk
AND
Loch Fyne Smokehouse
Ardkinglas
Argyll
Tel 01499 600217
www.loch-fyne.com

POTATOES
Knowes Farm Shop
By East Linton
East Lothian EH42 1XJ
Tel 01620 860010

SCOTCH PIES AND SAUSAGES
Stuart's of Buckhaven
19 Randolph Street
Buckhaven
Fife KY8 1AT
Tel 01592 713413

SMOKED GAME
Rannoch Smokery
Kinloch Rannoch
By Pitlochry
Perthshire PH16 5QD
Tel 0870 1601559
www.rannochsmokery.co.uk

**SMOKED AND FRESH FISH,
   AND SHELLFISH**
George Armstrong
80 Raeburn Place
Edinburgh EH4 1HH
Tel 0131 3152033

SMOKED SALMON
Shetland Smokehouse
Skeld, Shetland ZE2 9NL
Tel 01595 860203
www.shetlandsmokehouse.co.uk
AND
Inverawe Smokehouse
Taynuilt, Argyll PA35 1HU
Tel 01866 822446
www.smokedsalmon.co.uk

SOFT FRUITS
G. & G. Sinclair
West Craigie Farm
South Queensferry EH30 9TR
Tel 0131 3191048

(FARMED) VENISON
Fletchers Fine Foods,
Reediehill Farm
Auchtermuchty KY14 7HS
Tel 01337 828369
www.seriouslygoodvenison.co.uk

WHITE PUDDING
Ritchie's of Aultbea
55 Mellon Charles
Aultbea
Ross-shire IV22 2JL
Tel 01445 731040

Bibliography

An Isle called Hirte, Mary Harman (Maclean Press, 1997)
A Description of the Western Islands of Scotland circa 1695,
     and *A Description of the Occidental Isles of Scotland 1549*, Donald Munro (Birlinn, 2002)
Knee Deep in Claret, Billy Kay and Cailean Maclean (Auld Alliance, 1983)
Old Edinburgh Taverns, Marie W Stuart (Robert Hale, 1952)
Herring: a History of the Silver Darlings, Mike Smylie (Tempus, 2004)
The Scots and their Fish, G. W. Lockart (Birlinn, 1997)
The Scot and his Oats, G. W. Lockart (Luath Press 1983)
The Cookery Book of Lady Clark of Tillypronie (Southover Press, 1994)
The Scots Kitchen, F. Marian McNeill (Blackie & Son, 1953)
Traditional Scottish Cookery, Theodora Fitzgibbon (Mercat Press, 2004)
Scottish Cookery, Catherine Brown (Richard Drew, 1989)
Something about Mary, Mary Coghill (the Powell Family, 2004)
Sula the Seabird-hunters of Lewis, John Beatty (Michael Joseph, 1992)
The Life and Death of St Kilda, Tom Steel (HarperCollins, 1994)
A Journey to the Western Islands of Scotland & The Journal of a Tour to the Hebrides 1773,
     Samuel Johnson and James Boswell (Penguin Books, 1984)
The Antiquary, Sir Walter Scott (Oxford University Press, 2002)
Katharine Jane Ellice's Recipe Book, (National Library of Scotland, Invernessshire, 1846)
A New and Easy Method of Cookery, Elizabeth Cleland (National Library of Scotland, Edinburgh, 1755)
Margaret Stewart's Recipe Book 1799 (National Library of Scotland)
Mrs Johnston's Receipts (National Library of Scotland, Edinburgh, 1740)
Janet Maule's Recipe Book 1701 (National Library of Scotland)

Index